THIS I BELIEVE

Other books by E.F. Schumacher

SMALL IS BEAUTIFUL
A GUIDE FOR THE PERPLEXED
GOOD WORK

THIS I BELIEVE

 and other essays

E.F. Schumacher

A RESURGENCE BOOK

A Resurgence Book
first published in 1997
by Green Books Ltd
Foxhole, Dartington
Totnes, Devon TQ9 6EB, UK

Reprinted with corrections 1998

Distributed in the USA by
Chelsea Green Publishing Company
White River Junction, Vermont

Typeset in Sabon at Green Books

Printed by J.W. Arrowsmith Ltd
Bristol

A catalogue record for this book is
available from The British Library

ISBN 1 870098 66 8

The ideas and values of E.F. Schumacher live on
in the Schumacher Societies in the UK and USA,
which promote good economic practice, ecological
and spiritual values, and human-scale development.

For further details contact:
The Schumacher Society, Foxhole, Dartington
Totnes, Devon TQ9 6EB, UK

or

The E.F. Schumacher Society, 140 Jug End Lane
Great Barrington, MA 01230, USA

Contents

Acknowledgements

We would like to thank Mrs Verena Schumacher for kindly allowing this collection of articles by her late husband to be published.

The thirty-five articles by E.F. Schumacher that were published in *Resurgence* are as follows; those not included in this volume are shown in square brackets.

Industrialisation through Intermediate Technology Vol 1 No 2, July-Aug 1966; *Industrial Society* Vol 1 No 3, Sept-Oct 1966; [*The Economics of Intermediate Technology* Vol 1 No 7, May-June 1966]; *Man need not Starve* Vol 1 No 10, Nov-Dec 1967; *Buddhist Economics* Vol 1 No 11, Jan-Feb 196; *The New Economics* Vol 2 No 3, Sept-Oct 1968; *Industry & Morals* Vol 2 No 5, Jan-Feb 1969; *The Use of the Land* Vol 2 No 7, May-June 1969; *Healthy Development* Vol 2 No 8/9, July-Oct 1969; [*The Economics of Permanence* Vol 3 No 1, May-June 1970]; [*Modern Industry in the Light of the Gospel* Vol 3 No 6, Mar-Apr 1971]; [*Christian Responsibility in the present Economic and Inflationary Crisis* Vol 3 No 7, May-June 1971]; [*Numbers or Activities* Vol 4 No 5, Nov-Dec 1973]; [*Small, Simple and Non-Violent* Vol 4 No 6, Jan-Feb 1974] [*Education for Leisure and Wholesome Work* Vol 5 No 1, Mar-Apr 1974]; *Insane Work Cannot Produce a Sane Society* Vol 5 No 2, May-June 1974; *Western Europe's Energy Crisis* Vol 5 No 3, July-Aug 1974; *How to Abolish Land Speculation* Vol 5 No 4, Sept-Oct 1974; *Message from the Universe* Vol 5 No 5, Nov-Dec 1974; *No Future for Megapolis* Vol 5 No 6, Jan-Feb 1975; *Conscious Culture of Poverty* Vol 6 No 1, Mar-Apr 1975; [*On Inflation* Vol 6 No 2, May-June 1975]; *The Critical Question of Size* Vol 6 No 3, July-Aug 1975; *The Party is Over* Vol 6 No 4, Sept-Oct 1975; [*What Kind of India* Vol 6 No 5, Nov-Dec 1975]; *This I Believe...* Vol 7 No 1, Mar-Apr 1976; [*The Turn of the Tree* Vol 7 No 2, May-June 1976]; *Asia Undermined* Vol 7 No 3, July-Aug 1976; *Technology & Political Change* Vol 7 No 4, Sept-Oct 1976; *End of An Era* Volume 7 No 5, Nov-Dec 1976; *The Roots of Violence* Vol 7 No 6, Jan-Feb 1977; [*Science with Soul* Vol 8 No 1, Mar-Apr 1977]; [*City Patterns* Vol 8 No 2, May-June 1977]; [*Independence & Economic Development* Vol 8 No 3, July-Aug 1977]; *Public Funds for Voluntary Work* Vol 8 No 4, Sept-Oct 1977.

Foreword
by Satish Kumar

I met E. F. Schumacher in 1968 after reading his essay on Buddhist Economics. Nothing before and nothing since have I read by a Western economist which moved me so much. Here was a voice of wisdom and reason united. The moment I read his essay, I phoned him. "Come to my office at the National Coal Board and we will have lunch together." He took me to an Italian restaurant and we lunched and talked for two hours. It was instantly a meeting of minds, and the beginning of a relationship which was to last beyond his death.

When I took over the editorship of *Resurgence* in 1973, again I went to see Schumacher at his home in Caterham, Surrey. Although he had written occasional articles for *Resurgence* whilst John Papworth was Editor, I wanted to persuade him to write for every issue. When we had finished our business discussions, he gave me a guided tour of his garden and home. He was very pleased with his motorised wheelbarrow as an example of appropriate technology. He said, "When you get old like me, you need some power-assisted tools, but technology should not replace human input—rather, the role of technology is to aid human hands." He had just planted forty trees in his garden, and was very proud of them. "Silviculture and forest farming are the only way to safeguard our future and the health of the planet," he said.

When we returned to the house he showed me his hand-operated flourmill, which had two millstones for grinding flour for domestic use. "This is my pride and joy," he announced. "I grind wheat which I buy directly from the organic farm of Sam Mayall and bake bread for my family for the week. Bread made from freshly ground flour is vastly superior to other breads. So those who want the most nutritious bread must grind their own flour. Many people eat bread which has little more nutritional value than a paper serviette."

He believed that the decisions he made which affected everyday life were as important as his advice on policy matters to the National

Coal Board, where he was head of the Statistics Department.

As Schumacher talked, I felt that I was in the presence of a great man. Someone who could see the truth beyond received opinions. "Any fool can make things complicated, but it requires a genius to make things simple." He expressed his exasperation with our high technology society which makes life unnecessarily complicated.

He was sent by the British government to advise the government of Burma. Recalling his time there he said, "Within a few weeks of my arrival in Rangoon and after visiting a few villages and towns, I realised that the Burmese needed little advice from a Western economist like me. In fact we Western economists could learn a thing or two from the Burmese. They have a perfectly good economic system which has supported a highly developed religion and culture and produced not only enough rice for their own people but also a surplus for the markets of India."

"When I published my findings in Burma under the title of Buddhist Economics, a number of my economist colleagues said, 'Mr Schumacher, what does economics have to do with Buddhism?' " My answer was simply that economics without Buddhism is like sex without love. "Economics without spirituality can give you temporary and physical gratification, but it cannot provide an internal fulfilment. Spiritual economics brings service, compassion and relationships into equal play with profit and efficiency. We need both and we need them simultaneously."

Schumacher was one of the first Western economists who dared to put those two words—Buddhist and economics—together. This was an act of courage. When his fellow economists called him a crank, Schumacher took it with a sense of humour. He said, "What is wrong with being a crank? The crank is the part of the machine which creates revolution and it is very small. I am a small revolutionary! It is a compliment."

It was in Burma that he got the idea of intermediate technology. "The Buddha taught the value of the Middle Path. For instance, in agriculture many Third World countries still use sickle technology to harvest their crops. This could be called stage one. Whereas in the West we have the automated and highly sophisticated combine harvester, which has nearly eliminated the human element in farming altogether. This could be called stage ten. So I thought: what has happened to all the stages in between? This is my theory of the disappearing middle. As a consequence, I launched the Intermediate Technology Development Group to research and reintroduce some of those middle technologies which are human friendly, environment friendly and which render considerable help to farmers around the world without the depletion of resources and loss of employment that high technology involves."

At that time he had just published his first book, *Small is Beautiful*; he gave me a copy, eagerly explaining why he attached so much value to the question of smallness. "Industrial and technological advancement is obsessed with the economics of scale. As a result, huge bureaucracies, giant companies and enormous factories have come to be seen as the symbols of success. But the reality is that things are done according to the rules, and human relationships have become secondary. As giant technologies are anti-human, so are giant organisations. In big schools, pupils are reduced to numbers; in big hospitals, patients are reduced to numbers; in big factories, workers are reduced to numbers. Economics should serve the values of humanity and even the spiritual growth of human beings. In my view that cannot happen if our organisations are beyond a certain size. That is why I called my book *Small is Beautiful*." I had not heard this kind of philosophy in the West— and from an economist who had been through Oxford, *The Times*, and a nationalised industry.

From November 1973 to August 1977 he contributed twenty-three articles to *Resurgence*. When I phoned to discuss them, he listened carefully and was prepared to alter or shorten his pieces to fit the magazine. He was one of the easiest authors to work with, but he preferred a clean, clear layout for his articles. Once our adventurous Resurgence designer put a faint illustration as a background to the whole page. He didn't like that and said so. "The purpose of design is to make reading easier, not more difficult," he said.

It is a great pleasure to see a selection of his *Resurgence* articles now being put together in a book. Even though these articles were written at different times and appear to be disparate, there is a strong common theme throughout. This theme shows the total integration of the spiritual and material, inner and outer, ideal and real, visionary and practical. There is no dualism in the thoughts of E.F. Schumacher.

Hartland, 10th March 1997

Introduction
by Diana Schumacher

Fritz Schumacher, the economist-philosopher, was born in Bonn in 1911, lived the greater part of his life in England and died on a visit to Caux, Switzerland in September 1977. Although from a distinguished intellectual background, and having himself experienced a meteoric academic career in Germany, England and America before the age of 23, Schumacher always believed that an ounce of practice is worth a ton of theory, and also that "the slenderest knowledge that may be obtained of the higher things is more desirable than the most certain knowledge that may be obtained of lesser things". He complained that throughout his own school and university careers he had been given "maps of life and knowledge" on which "there was hardly a trace of many of the things I most cared about and that seemed to me of the greatest possible importance to the conduct of my life". He saw the need to provide his colleagues and audiences with philosophical maps related to actual reality. In the process, his life was one of constant challenges and questioning, including most of the basic assumptions on which Western economic and academic theory had been based. What are the 'laws' that govern the 'science' of economics? What is the true value of money? What is the relationship between time and money? What is the real worth of work? And of development?

Part of Schumacher's personal sorrow—but analytical strength and objectivity—lay in the fact that he remained an 'an outsider' for most of his life. Having mainly studied overseas between the two wars, he never fully integrated with his fellow students. His appointment as assistant professor of banking at the University of Columbia at the tender age of 23 only set him further apart. His early commercial assignments ranged from Wall Street to the City of London, to an independent and lucrative barter import-export enterprise run from Germany during the pre-war depression.

In 1937, owing to Hitler's frenzied ascendancy and his own feeling of the intellectual and political betrayal of Germany and its heritage by his nationalistic compatriots, he decided to abandon all social, family and business ties and to bring his young wife to London. He was certain that until Germany could be purged of the Nazis' evil presence there would be no peace in Europe; but that ultimately the reconstruction of Europe might be led from England. He hoped that he would then be in the vanguard of social and economic reform.

During the war, they faced the hostility of being regarded as German aliens. The family had to give up their home, and after being briefly interned, Schumacher worked as a farm labourer in Northamptonshire, before being hidden away doing government research at the Oxford Institute of Statistics. Immediately after the war he was appointed economic adviser to the Allied Control Commission, and was sent back to Germany where many of his relatives and friends regarded the now naturalised English family as traitors who had deserted the sinking ship. Although the family were again back in England from 1950 onwards (he was now Economic Advisor and Director of Statistics to the newly nation-alised National Coal Board), Schumacher's quest for patterns of sustainability took him all over the world. He had experienced poverty, social injustice and alienation first-hand, and felt that with his unique and practical background, he had something useful to contribute. As he once remarked, "I am a fellow without a father-land"—a sad acknowledgement for one who had taken patriotism and an extremely privileged social and academic heritage so much for granted.

At one stage or another, during his life in exile, Fritz questioned all traditional structures, whether intellectual, national, economic or religious. Until 1951 he remained a dedicated atheist, lecturing that religion and morality were mere products of history; they did not stand up to scientific examination and could be altered if inappro-priate. He was an idealist with a restless mind whose earliest values had been very modern based on the speed, measurement, efficien-cy and logic of the Western world which he inhabited. It was only much later that he understood that such criteria were too inflexible, and totally incompatible with the more subtle 'unconscious' rhythms of the natural world.

Highly cultured and courteous by upbringing, and adaptable by rigorous necessity, Schumacher remained an intellectually lone figure, but this continued to reinforce his objectivity. Different individuals or groups understood different aspects of his work, as it fitted into their own scheme of thinking. Few saw his vision as a whole. Most of his more radical social ideas for agricultural or economic reform, and his 'world improvement schemes' were either derided or at best discussed by those with influence, but were rarely developed in the ways he advocated.

His energetic and enquiring search for truth meant that his mind had of necessity to divest itself of cultural clutter and inherited academic baggage which might stand in the way. However this increased his ability to adapt from the high flying academic, to international businessman, fiscal researcher, financial adviser, camp internee, farm labourer, government policy researcher, translator, journalist and civil servant, as necessity demanded. He never failed to use each of his changes in fortune to learn as much as possible from the situation he was in, and to pursue his inner quest. As he commented in *Guide for the Perplexed*, "The art of living is always to make a good thing out of a bad thing. This then leads to seeing the world in a new light." He was never bitter and never gave way to despair. His life was a true expression of Gandhian non-violence (*ahimsa*); of finding a balance—or later, in Buddhist terms, of finding 'the middle way'.

During and immediately after the Second World War, Schumacher was invited to write for *The Observer*, *The Times*, *The Economist* and other journals under pseudonyms, the editors fearing that the German name would offend. Sometimes his ideas were appropriated by others, such as his contribution to the Marshall Plan of 1947 or to the Beveridge Report on Full Employment of 1944. Although he never received official recognition for his intellectual contributions to such prestigious schemes until almost the last decade of his life, this did not disquiet him. The most important aspect of all intellectual and research experience, in his view, was to get the necessary ideas implemented by whoever was able to effect them.

Schumacher always read prolifically. He was influenced by many different philosophers and thinkers—from Shakespeare to Shaw; from Marx to Einstein; from R.H. Tawney to Chairman Mao; from Adam Smith to J.M. Keynes; from Gurdjieff to Gandhi. Even as a commuter from suburban Caterham where he lived, to the National Coal Board headquarters in London's Victoria (where he worked from 1950 to 1970), he used all the train travelling time to study comparative religions. This period proved a most fruitful turning point in his inner life. He first studied notably those religions from the East, attended lectures and began to practice meditation. Gradually and reluctantly he came to relinquish the atheism of his youth and to admit to the possibility of a higher order of being. In both his active life and his inner life he essentially followed the Gandhian search for truth. This explains why, like Gandhi, his changing economic and metaphysical views (which sometimes seemed contradictory) chronologically mirrored his own spiritual struggles and developments. His speeches, articles and projects likewise reflected these changes from Marxism through Buddhism and eventually to Christianity.

In 1955, whilst working at the National Coal Board, Schumacher accepted a three-month assignment as Economic Development Adviser to the Government of the Union of Burma, where he immediately attached himself to a Buddhist monastery. He also discovered that the Burmese needed no economic development along Western lines. His report was not well received, but the experience proved yet another turning point in his spiritual and intellectual development. Burma brought together many of the separate strands in his life particularly relating to economic development in the third world (see chapter three on Buddhist Economics). It also opened the door to his later studies of Western religions, and eventually through Thomas Aquinas and the Early Church Fathers to Christianity. To the astonishment of Schumacher's Marxist and Buddhist friends alike, he was finally received into the Roman Catholic Church in 1971, six years before he died. It was a formal renouncement of his previously cherished views of the supremacy of the intellect and reason over the Christian virtues of compassion, forgiveness, unconditional love, the acknowledgement of a Divine Creator, and the integrity of all creation.

There was, after all, a transcendent 'vertical perspective' to life. After years of searching and inner struggles he had realised a way of bringing his lifelong paths of study and social concerns to a point of convergence and had reached his own spiritual homecoming.

In tandem with his job at the Coal Board, Schumacher also undertook an intensive programme of international travel, initially to give substance to his proposals to save the collapsing European coal industry, and to encourage independence from the Western world's industrial reliance on cheap oil imports from the Middle East. His aim was also to promote sustainable development strategies in the First and Third World alike, including the US, Latin America, Japan and Russia (although he never lived to see the end of the Cold War). Fuel and food he saw as the two basic necessities for survival and sustainability. All communities should strive to be self-sufficient in these as far as possible—otherwise they become economically and politically vulnerable. Unfortunately he was years ahead of his time, and few took much notice. Putting his theories into practice, his was one of the first UK houses have solar panels installed on its roof. He also personally became involved in sustainable agriculture, an enthusiasm which he claimed had its seeds in his work as a farm labourer. He spent much time on his organic garden, was a prominent member of the UK Soil Association, supported Men of the Trees, and was an unflagging advocate of tree-planting and forest farming schemes wherever he went. He lost no opportunity to warn against soil impoverishment, the erosion and ecological degradation following forest-felling schemes, or of economic dependence of agricultural systems based on monocultures, and oil-based chemical fertilisers.

In 1970, with a small group of committed colleagues including George McRobie from the National Coal Board, Schumacher founded the Intermediate Technology Development Group, a London-based charity dealing with technology transfer. The aim was to give practical 'tool aid', skills and education to poor rural communities in developing countries. With Indian colleagues, he also helped to set up in Lucknow the Appropriate Technology Development Association, working very much along the same lines. As can be seen, this was 'Buddhist economics' in practice. He had understood that Western aid to poor communities simply serves to increase their cultural and economic dependence, and to increase the gulf between rich and poor, young and old, even within their own societies. On the other hand, by respecting communities' own indigenous and cultural traditions, providing them with skills and upgraded tools, they will be enabled to achieve long term sustainability and security. This 'middle way' has gained increasing recognition over the past twenty-five years, particularly among the poor countries themselves. Both charities continue to flourish and develop today, and indeed the Intermediate Technology Development Group now has interlinked offices in six countries, serving many different regions.

Despite growing acclaim for Schumacher's projects, broadcasts, writings and public lectures during the 1960s, the real breakthrough and recognition only came with the publication in 1973 of his first book *Small is Beautiful: Economics as if People Mattered*. This was written in layman's terms, since it was mainly based on previous lectures and articles, but it somehow caught the spirit of the times. *Small is Beautiful* was not just about appropriate size. It articulated what millions of 'little people' world-wide subconsciously believed: that unlike any previous culture or civilisation, twentieth century western society, whether agricultural or industrial, was living artificially on the Earth's capital rather than on its income. Its lifeblood was the ever- increasing use of non-renewable resources primarily by the rich countries. Life could not continue sustainably on the increasing curve of production and consumption without material or moral restraint. Schumacher's simple yet provocative style of communication inspired many people to question the future and values of the marketeering, consumer society, and to make radical changes in their own lifestyles. It was, however, his personal commitment and dedication which kindled enthusiasm and the courage to change. This message of empowerment had unusual resonance world-wide, with people from President Carter of the USA, who summoned him to the White House in 1977, to countless thousands of dispossessed people in the Third World. The latter he encouraged to adhere to their traditional values, but also to find their own 'middle way' of sustainable development. He exhorted all to rely on people power and their own mental and physical inventiveness, rather than basing their futures on capital and energy-intensive technologies. The message still flies in the face of most prevailing economic policies today.

Schumacher's dictum was: "Occupy yourself with the things which can be changed". Any good practical action, however small, is always significant. Society must learn again to separate needs from wants; the quality of life from the quantity of consumption; wisdom from knowledge; production by the masses from mass production. He, along with Barbara Ward, was among the first economists to challenge the unqualified desirability of the growth concept. Overnight he was hailed as the guru of materialistic dissent. He has since been acclaimed as the true prophet of sustainable development—that little understood clarion cry of the 1990s. For Schumacher the concept of sustainability automatically places the spiritual and material well-being of the people involved at the forefront of all policy and decision-making.

A Guide for the Perplexed, outlining his deepest spiritual beliefs followed in 1977; other works were published posthumously. But *Small is Beautiful* remains the book by which Schumacher is generally remembered. The strength of his arguments still lie in his ability to address problems at the systems level, and to communicate solutions simply and practically. His message was an inclusive one, as can be seen from the different chapters in this book. Do not break down problems into isolated components but "look at the world and see it whole".

This I Believe covers many of the convergent themes of Schumacher's life. The first two sections outline his scepticism of Western economic giganticism, and the need to find a new economics related to human scale and sustainability. Chapters 6, 7 and 8 reinforce his views of the dignity and creativity of human work as the basis of a sane and productive society; of a new role for accountable voluntary agencies working in an active symbiosis with government agencies and the effectiveness and desirability of locally-based, bottom-up development models. Societies should aim to produce goods with 'eternal', rather than 'ephemeral' value to avoid a 'culture of poverty'. This is a direct challenge, of course, to our throw-away society, with its built-in obsolescence. His views on sustainable and non-polluting energy supplies as a basis of industrial, agricultural and environmental sustainability prevail throughout; as does the need to find new organisational structures compatible with the dignity of work, ownership, and the role of technology. The section on development gives practical proposals as to how to alleviate poverty, famine and the associated problems. Based on his own experience and projects, imaginative ideas for both urban and agricultural regeneration and community health are all to be found here. Finally, in the concluding chapters, Schumacher shares some of the deeper ecological and spiritual insights which have inspired his work, and which help us to understand where our thinking has gone astray, and how we can get back on the right path. The metaphysics of our materialism is now directly challenging the environment:

"The problem posed by environmental deterioration is not primarily a technical problem; if it were, it would not have arisen in its acutest form in the technologically most advanced societies. It does not stem from scientific or technical incompetence, or from insufficient scientific education, or from a lack of information, or from any shortage of trained manpower, or lack of money for research. It stems from the life-style of the modern world, which in turn arises from its most basic beliefs—its metaphysics, if you like."

It is only a complete metanoia in all departments of life, rather than engaging in an 'over-extending battle with symptoms' which will educate us to change sufficiently fundamentally, to avoid universal breakdown.

Twenty years after Schumacher's death, the wisdom, warnings and predictions contained in these controversial writings, are seen to be more relevant than ever. Some of his views, such as those on total accounting and accountability, taking not only monetary but environmental and non-renewable resource costs into consideration in policy-making, are now at last creeping on to the political agenda. Also some of the international development organisations are beginning to look for more low-cost, or micro-credit schemes and ways in which to address poverty at a local level. Nevertheless the trend towards ecological globalisation, the vast growth of mega cities, mass unemployment, unsustainable agricultural and industrial patterns, and increasing environmental degradation and social violence demonstrate that his 'maps' are still not being understood, or interpreted correctly by those in a position to change policies. There is now an even more urgent need to revisit some of these fundamental prerequisites for sustainability—namely the transcendence of moral values; the equality and dignity of all people in the eyes of God; the integrity of human work as the resource base of any economy; the value of local communities; and the need for decentralised decision-making and self-sufficiency wherever practicable.

There is always a great danger to freeze a human icon, such as Gandhi or Schumacher, in the situation of their time, and not to allow for the fact that their own ideas would be constantly changing and moving on with changed circumstances. They would be finding new solutions to new phenomena as they arose, and would be practising the art of 'living in the present moment', and encouraging others to do likewise. The revolutions in information technology, virtual reality and genetic engineering, were undoubtedly issues which have arisen during the last twenty years, and which would have occupied Schumacher's attention insofar as they affect our overall human condition. Although he repeatedly warned of the inherent dangers of nuclear power, and the probability of a Chernobyl-style accident occurring, global warming had not been scientifically acknowledged as environmentally threatening at the time of his death. However, most of the problems which Schumacher addresses here, are unfortunately still with us, and many of these have since been exacerbated.

It is now up to a new generation to arm itself with the necessary knowledge and moral courage to find its own solutions to contemporary crises and to build peace at all levels. It is important to form partnerships with those individuals who will share the challenge of change and who are ready to make use of the same 'maps'. As Schumacher said in *Good Work*,

> "I certainly never feel discouraged. I can't myself raise the winds which might blow us, or this ship into a better world. But I can at least put up the sail, so that when the wind comes I can catch it."

We are now, as then, all in the same boat! I am sure that readers will find in this book a treasury of useful insights and tools for change, and as such it may be seen as a fitting sequel to *Small is Beautiful*.

Godstone, June 1997

SETTING THE SCENE

~ Chapter I ~
The Party is Over

To JUDGE BY THE FLOOD of public utterances on the state of the nation, we are in the later phases of a bad economic crisis which has a number of disagreeable features, inflation being the worst. We are told that we must cut the rate of inflation by half, so as to be more nearly in line with our main competitors and to put ourselves in a good position to benefit from the upswing in the world economy confidently predicted for early next year; that we shall then be able to balance our international accounts, even start repaying our monstrous debts, and, once the North Sea oil really starts flowing in bulk, get back onto the happy road of economic growth. All of which makes me burst out in verse:

> When GNP begins to grow once more
> We shall be even happier than before.

This kind of optimism is enough to depress even the staunchest heart. Where shall we be when we are back on this 'happy road?' Surely we shall be in a more dangerous and insupportable position than we were a few years ago. The three-fold crisis—the crisis of resources, the ecological crisis, and the social crisis—will still be with us, in an accentuated form. Everything will be even more brittle and vulnerable.

The present situation, I am certain, has nothing in common with any previous 'depression' or 'recession'—except of course some of the symptoms like unemployment. It is not part of a cycle, is not a 'correction' or a 'shake-out' or anything of this sort: *It is the end of an era.* As Barbara Ward put it very simply a year or so ago: "The party is over."

What sort of a party was it? It was a party mainly for a small minority of countries and for a small (though growing) minority within these countries, and most of the people who provided the goods and services to keep the party going were more or less left out. We allowed ourselves to be entertained by three illusions:

First, there was the illusion of an inexhaustible supply of cheap fuels and raw materials.

Second, there was the illusion of an almost equally inexhaustible supply of workers willing to do boring, repetitive, soul-destroying work for very modest rewards.

Third, there was the illusion that Science and Technology would soon, very soon indeed, make everybody so rich that no problems remained except what on earth to do with all our leisure and wealth.

These illusionary entertainers, who made the party what it was, all three of them, have left, have completely vanished: they had cast a spell over us, had taken us on a trip. Every day now it seems more incredible that we were ever taken in by them and believed what they told us. We are waking up—and see a great deal of debris around us—but the spell is still there in a subtle kind of way: most of what we say and do is still based on the implicit assumption that the three entertainers will soon return and the party will be resumed.

In fact, we all *know* that the three entertainers will *not* return; that the party *is* over. But since it would be too strenuous and perhaps too upsetting to think of and evolve something new, a new life-style for instance, we prefer to indulge in that great and re-assuring psychological exercise which has aptly been called 'the refusal of consciousness'.

This deplorable condition is by no means confined to Britain. I have just seen the verbatim report of a very high-level discussion meeting held in Germany a few months ago—not only Chancellor Schmidt but also the president of the German Central Bank were among the participants, along with internationally famous economists, diplomats, and administrators—and there was not even the faintest sign of any other wish than to return, as quickly as possible, to the trends of the 1950s and 1960s, as if the present crises were the result of some kind of international traffic accident and in no way the inevitable outcome of these very trends.

A similar 'refusal of consciousness' can be observed in other fields, such as the natural sciences. Here, too, 'the party is over'. It was a very peculiar party, in fact an orgy of nihilism, a celebration of the allegedly scientific findings that there are no values, no purposes, no meanings; that the human race is nothing but a cosmic accident (which may well have occurred also in other parts of the Universe); and that mindless 'matter' or 'energy' is the ultimate reality. While the party was still in full swing, perhaps the most revered exhibit was the Second Law of Thermodynamics, or the Law of Entropy, which asserts that everything always 'runs down' (unless it is feeding parasitically on something else) and that the whole Universe must inevitably end in death and dissolution. Theodore Roszak takes issue with the scientists on this point and asks:

"Why have they done such a zany thing; Perhaps it is because entropy is nihilistic; it points towards universal death and dissolution, and so supports the assumption of an alien, humanly meaningless universe, a universe which is impassively, impersonally there for detached study and manipulation. . . To proceed analytically from the whole to the parts, to reduce qualities to quantities, to exclude final causes, to assume the radical objectivity of nature: these are not so many hypotheses up for proof. All this, taken together, is science—or at least science as we have known it in the West since the days of Galileo."

Everywhere now there are indications that science has reached the end of this particular era. The evidence is coming in from all sides: that physics and chemistry cannot account for more than a kind of 'substratum' of phenomena and must be seen *as being in the service of higher forces* when it comes to matters like life, intelligence, and consciousness. This evidence, of course, has never been lacking to natural philosophers and countless others who would never think of themselves as possessing more than ordinary common sense; but it is now coming from the scientists themselves: as they are looking more closely at nature they are finding it impossible to fit nature into their materialistic framework of thought.

The result is a rapidly increasing flow of publications of which *The Secret Life of Plants* by Peter Tompkins and Christopher Bird may be taken as a fair representative. They report on innumerable experiments which cannot be explained by orthodox science. They also, incidentally, are full of horrifying stories of persecution suffered by people of genius whose scientific findings were too unorthodox to be acceptable. (The subjects where the greatest amount of intolerance is to be found seem to be Medicine and Agriculture.)

What is so peculiar and, it seems, unacceptable about these experiments is that they attain substantial results nonviolently, that is to say, with only the minutest inputs of energy or other substances—in total contrast to the technologies derived from orthodox science which tend to be extraordinarily violent and require very high inputs, particularly of energy.

The literature now available contains so many indications of new possibilities of healing, for instance, or of growing things in agriculture and horticulture that one should have thought the scientists in these fields would be at the height of intellectual ferment and excitement and would be most impatient to undertake work along these novel lines. However, nothing of the sort is happening, except with a few intrepid pioneers. The scientific establishment practices the art of 'refusal of consciousness' with perfection.

All the same, there is reason for optimism. The pressures are mounting, and the defences built up by the refusal of consciousness are likely to give way before long. Once we understand the meaning of our economic crisis we shall know what needs to be done, and once we understand the meaning of our scientific crisis we shall be able to find ways of doing it.

It is, of course, necessary that we should bother our heads about inflation and all the other ephemeral problems that bother us. But we shall not ensure our survival by doing so. Survival will depend on our ability to overcome the 'refusal of consciousness' which defends totally outdated philosophies of 'economic progress' and 'scientific truth' as if they were (to quote Bertrand Russell) "if not quite beyond dispute. . . yet so nearly certain, that no philosophy that rejects them can hope to stand." It will be recalled that Russell came to the conclusion that "only on the firm foundation of unyielding despair can the soul's habitation henceforth be safely built."

Those who realise that in economics as well as in science we have come to the end of an era, have no cause for 'unyielding despair'. As the old dispensation dies away, the new one is already prepared. But it will take a lot of honest work to realise the possibilities which are now opening up.

Vol 6 No 4, Sept-Oct 1975

Chapter 2

End of an Era

AN ERA HAS COME TO AN END. There is the end of a certain phase in the thinking of Western humanity. We have discovered ourselves now to be in a very, very deep spiritual crisis. An era which has been dominated by Cartesian thinking and which has lasted for some 250 or 300 years, has seen unbelievable developments in science and technology. This era is now drawing to a close. Having worked out the consequences of this type of thinking, we find it makes us spiritually bankrupt. This thinking can be called 'preferring science to wisdom'. To illustrate it, here are two quotations. One comes from Aristotle via Thomas Aquinas. The other is from Huygens, following Descartes. The first one, which is the traditional wisdom of mankind, says, "The slenderest knowledge that may be obtained of the highest things is more desirable than the most certain knowledge obtained of lesser things." The second quotation, this time from the 17th Century, says, "What gravity is; what heat, cold, the attraction of the magnet, light, colours are; what elements go to make up air, water, fire or other bodies; what the purpose of respiration in animals is; how metal, stones and plants develop; of all these things little or nothing is yet known. There is, however, nothing in the world, the knowledge of which would be more desirable and more useful."

The total contrast is clear. Until the 17th Century they said that even the slightest, vaguest knowledge of the highest things was infinitely more desirable than the most precise knowledge of material things. Suddenly, there is a change and it is stated that there is nothing more desirable or useful in the world than the knowledge of material things. There is no longer a distinction between 'higher' and 'lower' things but only the thought of usefulness, desirability derived from usefulness. And so there has followed an era of violent dogmatism, a dogmatism which excludes from what may be considered real or scientifically acceptable everything except that which can be weighed and dealt with by that very small, useful instrument we call reason.

This change in the way of thinking has to be laid at the door of so-called 'scientific development'. The senses for enjoyment count no longer as an instrument for gaining knowledge. The feelings, affection, love, don't count any more. Character and will—these are both out. And so everything in reality, every subject, whether it is politics, economics, or any particular science becomes an isolated and separate system, because the only thing that henceforth is acceptable is what Descartes called "clear, certain and distinct ideas" and there is nothing really clear, certain and distinct unless you can put it into mathematical terms. Theology is out; metaphysics is out; art is sometimes alright; and ethics is just anybody's opinion; because what cannot be measured, what cannot be turned into mathematical terms, can certainly not be described as "clear, certain and distinct ideas". This is the Cartesian Universe which we have inherited, inside which we were brought up; this is still what fills most of our being, because that is the way we have been educated, a dumb Universe, or, to quote Shakespeare, "a tale told by an idiot, full of sound and fury, signifying nothing". Bertrand Russell, with his great brain, came to the conclusion that this was a dumb universe and that only an attitude of unyielding despair was intellectually honest. And books are still being published which tell us that this is so, and that anybody who denies it, anyone who sees any meaning in anything is just not abreast of modern knowledge.

Mystery, of course, is out altogether. It is almost a term of abuse and so we have lost this remarkable ability, this paradoxical ability, namely, the science of mystery, the knowledge of things that we cannot understand. Those who are theologians know the negative theology, which is a very high science and which is built upon knowing that we don't know; it is asserted that once we know we don't know, then we really can learn something about these highest things. A great Christian saint said, "My night allows the light to enter." This is not just a matter of religion—it's a matter that permeates our whole life—namely, the extent to which we can acquire the knowledge of non-knowledge, the tolerance of non-knowledge, the certainty of certain things that cannot be known; and so we develop certain ways of dealing with the unknown. This is a thought which is intolerable today. And so we pretend to ourselves that we know most things about the future, and that is a certain way of maximising our mistakes!

This is the era that is now coming to an end. It has also been described as the 'reign of quantity'. I learned a lesson during the war when I was a farm labourer up in Northamptonshire and one of my jobs every morning before breakfast was to go up a hill to a field nearby and count the cattle. So I trotted there, half asleep, and counted thirty-two and then I went down to the farm, touched my cap to the bailiff and said, "Yes, sir, thirty-two", and he said, "Go and have your breakfast." One day, when I arrived there, there was an old farmer standing at the gate and he said, "Young man, what do you do here every morning?" I said, "Nothing much, I just count the cattle." He shook his old head and said, "If you count them every day, they won't flourish." So I went back, murmuring to myself, "Those country yokels! How stupid can you get!" I mean, I am a professional statistician—he didn't know that. One day I came up there and I counted; I counted again and again, and there were only thirty-one. I wanted my breakfast so I went down and said to the bailiff, "There are only thirty-one." He was very angry and said, "Have your breakfast—we'll go up there after breakfast." We did and searched the place and, under one of the bushes, was a dead beast. I said to myself, "Wait a minute—why have I been here every morning counting them? That hasn't stopped that beast dying, has it? Maybe that old farmer had a point here which I missed." Perhaps he didn't put it very cleverly, "If you count them every day, they won't flourish!" What he may have meant was that if you train your mind on the quantity of them, you won't stop them dying. What does the quantity matter? What could have happened if I hadn't counted? A beast might have strayed away, but somebody would have brought it back. No, I ought to have looked for the qualitative factor, looked at every beast to see whether she was alright, whether she had a sheen on her coat, and so on. I ought to have been able to go back to the bailiff and say, "Oh, they seem alright except that one looks a bit mangy." Then we would have gone up and done something sensible. Quantity had got the better of me and had filled my mind instead of what really mattered, which is the quality of things.

My attention was later drawn to a piece of writing by Sir James Frazer, the author of *The Golden Bough*, who with his fantastic diligence had also dug up all sorts of traditional stories which he compiled in a little volume called *The Sin of Statistics*. He reports surprisingly from a variety of old traditions from right around the globe this ever-present attitude against counting, against the quantitative approach. Those who know their Bible will know that it was King David who first introduced a census and you will recollect that Jehovah was utterly furious and gave him the choice between three ghastly punishments. The old Jews were quite capable of arguing back, "I have done no wrong; what's the matter?" David, however, didn't argue. He just chose one of the three punishments because it would be over the quickest. He took the point; it was wrong to do this counting. If this were only in the Old Testament, you might say it is one of the peculiarities of the old Jews, but it comes from the Red Indians, the Eskimos, from everywhere—the sin of statistics. Sir James Frazer wrote about it with the arrogance of the 19th century, just as if he were saying, "Isn't that funny?" and the same kind of attitude prevails still. But after my little experience with the dead beast, I didn't think it was funny any more. I thought that I must take this very, very seriously. The purely quantitative approach misses out on everything that really matters and the age that is now drawing to a close has embraced this because, of course, in the material world this has a certain power. There is nothing wrong with it, provided it is counter-balanced by an understanding of what really matters, and that is something quite different.

In short, all this traditional wisdom was rejected in order to have what promised to be an easy and comfortable time. And, of course, we got the exact opposite, a totally meaningless time. And how opposite it is one can learn most easily if one moves over into the most advanced society that we have today, which is the United States, where the standard of living is still very much higher than that of Britain and the people are also very much more unhappy.

If it is true that this era is now coming to an end, we might ask, "Who has been instrumental in bringing this era to an end?" and the answer is disconcerting. It is not the theologians, not the Churches, not the thinkers, not the philosophers, not the academics, by and large. No, at this level, the only people that I can identify who have really struggled, are the ones who have gone to the extreme end of the Cartesian development—the physicists. The physicists have been asking the right question, 'What does it all mean?' and they have been writing for the past thirty years now really the most challenging philosophical books that have appeared in the West. That is one group. Perhaps this is the way human development takes place. We have to go to an extreme before understanding that we are on the wrong path.

The other group by whom the end of this era is being prepared are, in fact, the 'hippies', the sort of counter-culture, very often long-haired people—they are the people who are insisting on simple truths—such a simple truth as 'Make love, not war'. There is an interesting book which I do not agree with in its entirety, called *The Greening of America* by Charles Reich, which tells how suddenly, through the concrete, new green little plants are appearing, most of them weeds, but at least they have got through the concrete. These are the signs of a new era.

Also, of course, from quite another angle, there are people to whom we have every reason to be extremely grateful, like the OPEC countries, who have called the bluff of an economic system that assumes that the non-renewable materials like fossil fuels can be used at a rate that doubles every ten years.

There remains, of course, always the question of what we can do about it, when we have got this sort of general diagnosis. A lot of people want to rush into action, but it is still necessary to insist that the first act of doing is a real effort to understand, to sort these things out in one's own little mind. I find this very disconcerting. I encountered quite recently a fellow in the United States, who had done good work bringing things back to the human scale and then he published a journal and half of one number was full of some absolutely fantastic ideas of establishing living quarters out in space, each satellite for 10,000 people, with a technology that just takes your breath away, and some fragmentary people, so-called scientists, say all this is possible, if only we want to do it. Again this is a total aberration, a total cessation of the understanding which is gradually increasing of what the things are that really matter.

One of the most pertinent sentences in the Gospels is at the beginning of the Fourth Gospel, where it says, "In the beginning was the Word", but then one must say, "Read on, read on". It didn't stop there. The Word had to become incarnate, come down, become flesh and dwell among us. And that has a lot to do with the doing that is now necessary. Too often we communicate at the level of the word, and we don't change the world if we leave it there; unless the word, our message, our understanding, becomes incarnate, becomes flesh and dwells among us, nothing happens. This is a very deep insight of Christianity—that unless the word comes into the material world and becomes flesh, nothing happens. How then can we incarnate our good intentions, our insights, our new philosophy which is gradually growing in ourselves? The moment it becomes incarnate, no matter how modestly, it will become a much healthier plant inside us. And here I think everybody will make their own selection. I have chosen three kinds of actions for myself, as I encountered them on my own road—I am not suggesting that these are the only things that matter.

Firstly, we all need to realise that we need a different attitude to nature and we must practise a different attitude to nature in our gardening, our horticultural and agricultural activities. This is a very deep matter, not just a utilitarian matter. What has grown up, particularly over the past 30 years, is no longer a friendly co-operation with nature, but a battle against nature, a battle in which, if by chance we win it, we will find ourselves on the losing side. The much-praised modern agriculture has no long-term future, and there are material facts to support such a view. It has been worked out repeatedly now in the United States but also in Britain by Gerald Leach. This modern system of food production is so dependent on fossil fuels, primarily natural gas and oil, that if we thought we could feed the whole of humankind, some 4,000 million people, with this system of green revolution agriculture, we would find that all known resources would be absorbed by agriculture alone within less than 30 years. Now this knowledge is gradually dribbling into the heads of our masters. I was interested to see that, at an International Agricultural Conference, the head of the Royal Agricultural College, Sir Emrys Jones, told the young people there, aged about twenty or twenty-two, "Now, you watch it. By the time of your fifiteth birthday, you may have to farm without the help of oil and this means without the help of artificial fertilizer. And it's no good," he said, "sitting back and saying it is a wonderful system. The process of improving things by intensification, which has worked hitherto will not work in the future. By the time you are fifty, you will need a different farming system altogether." I am not aware that he told them what this different system would be, so he may have left them a little disconcerted. But the different system exists; it has, however, been dismissed hitherto as the 'muck and mystery' approach to agriculture, which I never took as an insult, because after all, muck and mystery is a pretty good definition of life in general. But here is an alternative system of agriculture which can be permanent.

Secondly, we have systematically to get rid of the idea, "the bigger, the better", and to understand that there is a certain measure in things that is right; beyond that or below that it is wrong. The beauty of smallness may be defined as that of the human scale. The beauty of it is (and each one of us ought to experiment with his hands) that at the right scale, you can introduce the TLC factor. Now TLC is the best fertilizer ever discovered and you can't buy it. It means Tender Loving Care. It is quite amazing what that can do and it is equally amazing what a mess you get into when it is organised out of the system. Take the National Health Service. When it began, there was great idealism that we, as a community, would look after one another and leave money out of it, and the new National Health Service inherited, as it were, from previous time, a great deal of TLC. But now, after 30 years, the thing has become more and more organised, more and more systematic, more and more quantified, measured and mechanised, and TLC has gone out of it. It's gone! There are certainly still human beings who want to practise TLC, but they must practise it against the system and so the system becomes quite unbelievably expensive. And also, it misses the point—it is not a National Health Service; it's a sort of anti-disease Fire Fighting Service. It has nothing at all to do with health any more. And this permeates the whole welfare system of the western world now. We are faced with the phenomenon that the richest city in the world, New York, is on the point of bankruptcy, and it is because the welfare system has become so inordinately expensive. Huge modern bureaucracies never achieve anything. They just amble along; the problems don't become smaller, they become bigger and bigger. If we think that we can solve things by monster size, we are just mistaken. Our problems today will be solved when we realise that we have to structure our organisations so that TLC, this most wonderful thing, which is also as satisfying to the giver as it is to the recipient, can again come into action. It is absolutely necessary and indeed inevitable, if we want to survive, to bring in many more activities back into the home, where homes still exist, and it is encouraging to see that there are now in various countries all sorts of movements to produce the technology which makes it possible to bring these things back into the home.

So the third kind of action is to produce a new technology. When I say, "The Word must become flesh", I refer to this kind of endeavour to bring our technology back on to a path that has the threefold virtue of health, beauty and permanence instead of the violence and giantism in which we now indulge.

From a talk given to the Iona Community
Vol 7 No 5, Nov-Dec 1976

ECONOMICS

Chapter 3

Buddhist Economics

'RIGHT LIVELIHOOD' IS ONE OF THE REQUIREMENTS of the Buddha's Noble Eightfold Path. It is clear, therefore, that there must be such a thing as Buddhist Economics.

Buddhist countries, at the same time, have often stated that they wish to remain faithful to their heritage. So Burma: "The New Burma sees no conflict between religious values and economic progress. Spiritual health and material well-being are not enemies: they are natural allies."[1] Or: "We can blend successfully the religious and spiritual values of our heritage with the benefits of modern technology."[2] Or: "We Burmans have a sacred duty to conform both our dreams and our acts to our faith. This we shall ever do."[3]

All the same, such countries invariably assume that they can model their economic development plans in accordance with modern economics, and they call upon modern economists from so-called advanced countries to advise them, to formulate the policies to be pursued, and to construct the grand design for development, the Five-Year Plan or whatever it may be called. No one seems to think that a Buddhist way of life would call for Buddhist economics, just as the modern materialist way of life has brought forth modern economics.

Economists themselves, like most specialists, normally suffer from a kind of metaphysical blindness, assuming that theirs is a science of absolute and invariable truths, without any presuppositions. Some go as far as to claim that economic laws are as free from 'metaphysics' or 'values' as the law of gravitation. We need not, however, get involved in arguments of methodology. Instead, let us take some fundamentals and see what they look like when viewed by a modern economist and a Buddhist economist.

There is universal agreement that the fundamental source of wealth is human labour. Now, the modern economist has been brought up to consider 'labour' or work as little more than a necessary evil. From the point of view of the employer, it is in any case simply an item of cost, to be reduced to a minimum if it cannot be eliminated altogether, say by automation. From the point of view of the workman, it is a 'disutility'; to work is to make a sacrifice of one's leisure and comfort, and wages are a kind of compensation for the sacrifice. Hence the ideal from the point of view of the employer is to have output without employees, and the ideal from the point of view of the employee is to have income without employment.

The consequences of these attitudes both in theory and in practice are, of course, extremely far-reaching. If the ideal with regard to work is to get rid of it, every method that 'reduces the work load' is a good thing. The most potent method, short of automation, is the so-called 'division of labour', and the classical example is the pin factory eulogised in Adam Smith's *Wealth of Nations*. Here it is not a matter of ordinary specialization, which mankind has practised from time immemorial, but of dividing up every complete process of production into minute parts, so that the final product can be produced at great speed without anyone having had to contribute more than a totally insignificant and, in most cases, unskilled movement of his limbs.

The Buddhist point of view takes the function of work to be at least threefold: to give a man a chance to utilize and develop his faculties; to enable him to overcome his ego-centredness by joining with other people in a common task; and to bring forth the goods and services needed for a becoming existence. Again, the consequences that flow from this view are endless. To organize work in such a manner that it becomes meaningless, boring, stultifying, or nerve-racking for the worker would be little short of criminal; it would indicate a greater concern with goods than with people, an evil lack of compassion and a soul-destroying degree of attachment to the most primitive side of this worldly existence. Equally, to strive for leisure as an alternative to work would be considered a complete misunderstanding of one of the basic truths of human existence, namely, that work and leisure are complementary parts of the same living process and cannot be separated without destroying the joy of work and the bliss of leisure.

From the Buddhist point of view, there are therefore two types of mechanization which must be clearly distinguished: one that enhances a man's skill and power and one that turns the work of

man over to a mechanical slave, leaving man in a position of having to serve the slave. How to tell the one from the other? "The
craftsman himself," says Ananda Coomaraswamy, a man equally
competent to talk about the Modern West as the Ancient East, "the
craftsman himself can always, if allowed to, draw the delicate distinction between the machine and the tool. The carpet loom is a
tool, a contrivance for holding warp threads at a stretch for the pile
to be woven round them by the craftsmen's fingers; but the power
loom is a machine, and its significance as a destroyer of culture lies
in the fact that it does the essentially human part of the work."[4] It
is clear, therefore, that Buddhist economics must be very different
from the economics of modern materialism, since the Buddhist sees
the essence of civilization not in a multiplication of wants but in
the purification of human character. Character, at the same time, is
formed primarily by a man's work. And work, properly conducted
in conditions of human dignity and freedom, blesses those who do
it and equally their products. The Indian philosopher and
economist J. C. Kumarappa sums the matter up as follows:

> "If the nature of the work is properly appreciated and applied,
> it will stand in the same relation to the higher faculties as food
> is to the physical body. It nourishes and enlivens the higher man
> and urges him to produce the best he is capable of. It directs his
> freewill along the proper course and disciplines the animal in
> him into progressive channels. It furnishes an excellent back-
> ground for man to display his scale of values and develop his
> personality."[5]

If a man has no chance of obtaining work he is in a desperate
position, not simply because he lacks an income but because he
lacks this nourishing and enlivening factor of disciplined work
which nothing can replace. A modern economist may engage in
highly sophisticated calculations on whether full employment
'pays' or whether it might be more 'economic' to run an economy
at less than full employment so as to ensure a greater mobility of
labour, a better stability of wages, and so forth. His fundamental
criterion of success is simply the total quantity of goods produced
during a given period of time. "If the marginal urgency of goods is
low," says Professor Galbraith in *The Affluent Society*, "then so is
the urgency of employing the last man or the last million men in

the labour force." And again: "If. . . we can afford some unemployment in the interest of stability—a proposition, incidentally, of
impeccably conservative antecedents—then we can afford to give
those who are unemployed the goods that enable them to sustain
their accustomed standard of living."[6]

From a Buddhist point of view, this is standing the truth on its
head by considering goods as more important than people and consumption as more important than creative activity. It means shift-
ing the emphasis from the worker to the product of work, that is,
from the human to the sub-human, a surrender to the forces of evil.
The very start of Buddhist economic planning would be a planning
for full employment, and the primary purpose of this would in fact
be employment for everyone who needs an 'outside' job: it would
not be the maximization of employment nor the maximization of
production. Women, on the whole, do not need an 'outside' job,
and the large-scale employment of women in offices or factories
would be considered a sign of serious economic failure. In particular, to let mothers of young children work in factories while the
children run wild would be as uneconomic in the eyes of a
Buddhist economist as the employment of a skilled worker as a sol-
dier in the eyes of a modern economist.

While the materialist is mainly interested in goods, the Buddhist
is mainly interested in liberation. But Buddhism is 'The Middle
Way' and therefore in no way antagonistic to physical well-being.
It is not wealth that stands in the way of liberation but the attachment to wealth, not the enjoyment of pleasurable things but the
craving for them. The keynote of Buddhist economics, therefore, is
simplicity and non-violence. From an economist's point of view,
the marvel of the Buddhist way of life is the utter rationality of
its pattern—amazingly small means leading to extraordinarily
satisfactory results.

For the modern economist this is very difficult to understand. He
is used to measuring the 'standard of living' by the amount of annual
consumption, assuming all the time that a man who consumes more
is 'better off' than a man who consumes less. A Buddhist economist
would consider this approach excessively irrational: since consumption is merely a means to human well-being, the aim should be
to obtain the maximum of well-being with the minimum of consumption. Thus, if the purpose of clothing is a certain amount of

temperature comfort and an attractive appearance, the task is to attain this purpose with the smallest possible effort, that is, with the smallest annual destruction of cloth and with the help of designs that involve the smallest possible input of toil. The less toil there is, the more time and strength is left for artistic creativity. It would be highly uneconomic, for instance, to go in for complicated tailoring, like the modern West, when a much more beautiful effect can be achieved by the skilful draping of uncut material. It would be the height of folly to make material so that it should wear out quickly and the height of barbarity to make anything ugly, shabby or mean. What has just been said about clothing applies equally to all other human requirements. The ownership and the consumption of goods is a means to an end, and Buddhist economics is the systematic study of how to attain given ends with the minimum means.

Modern economics, on the other hand, considers consumption to be the sole end and purpose of all economic activity, taking the factors of production—land, labour, and capital—as the means. The former, in short, tries to maximize human satisfactions by the optimal pattern of consumption, while the latter tries to maximize consumption by the optimal pattern of productive effort. It is easy to see that the effort needed to sustain a way of life which seeks to attain the optimal pattern of consumption is likely to be much smaller than the effort needed to sustain a drive for maximum consumption. We need not be surprised, therefore, that the pressure and strain of living is very much less in, say, Burma than it is in the United States, in spite of the fact that the amount of labour-saving machinery used in the former country is only a minute fraction of the amount used in the latter.

Simplicity and non-violence are obviously closely related. The optimal pattern of consumption, producing a high degree of human satisfaction by means of a relatively low rate of consumption, allows people to live without great pressure and strain and to fulfil the primary injunction of Buddhist teaching: "Cease to do evil; try to do good." As physical resources are everywhere limited, people satisfying their needs by means of a modest use of resources are obviously less likely to be at each other's throats than people depending upon a high rate of use. Equally, people who live in highly self-sufficient local communities are less likely to get involved in large-scale violence than people whose existence depends on world-wide systems of trade.

From the point of view of Buddhist economics, therefore, production from local resources for local needs is the most rational way of economic life, while dependence on imports from afar and the consequent need to produce for export to unknown and distant peoples is highly uneconomic and justifiable only in exceptional cases and on a small scale. Just as the modern economist would admit that a high rate of consumption of transport services between a man's home and his place of work signifies a misfortune and not a high standard of life, so the Buddhist economist would hold that to satisfy human wants from far-away sources rather than from sources nearby signifies failure rather than success. The former might take statistics showing an increase in the number of ton/miles per head of the population carried by a country's transport system as proof of economic progress, while to the latter—the Buddhist economist—the same statistics would indicate a highly undesirable deterioration in the *pattern* of consumption.

Another striking difference between modern economics and Buddhist economics arises over the use of natural resources. Bertrand de Juvenal, the eminent French political philosopher, has characterized 'Western man' in words which may be taken as a fair description of the modern economist:

> "He tends to count nothing as an expenditure, other than human effort; he does not seem to mind how much mineral matter he wastes and, far worse, how much living matter he destroys. He does not seem to realise at all that human life is a dependent part of an ecosystem of many different forms of life. As the world is ruled from towns where men are cut off from any form of life other than human, the feeling of belonging to an ecosystem is not revived. This results in a harsh and improvident treatment of things upon which we ultimately depend, such as water and trees."[7]

The teaching of the Buddha, on the other hand, enjoins a reverent and non-violent attitude not only to all sentient beings but also, with great emphasis, to trees. Every follower of the Buddha ought to plant a tree every few years and look after it until it is safely established, and the Buddhist economist can demonstrate without difficulty that the universal observance of this rule would result in a high rate of genuine economic development independent of any foreign aid. Much of the economic decay of South-East Asia (as of many other parts of the world) is undoubtedly due to a heedless and shameful neglect of trees.

Modern economics does not distinguish between renewable and non-renewable materials, as its very method is to equalize and quantify everything by means of a money price. Thus, taking various alternative fuels, like coal, oil, wood or water power: the only difference between them recognized by modern economics is relative cost per equivalent unit. The cheapest is automatically the one to be preferred, as to do otherwise would be irrational and 'uneconomic'. From a Buddhist point of view, of course, this will not do; the essential difference between non-renewable fuels like coal and oil on the one hand and renewable fuels like wood and water-power on the other cannot be simply overlooked. Non-renewable goods must be used only if they are indispensable, and then only with the greatest care and the most meticulous concern for conservation. To use them heedlessly or extravagantly is an act of violence, and while complete non-violence may not be attainable on this earth, there is none the less an ineluctable duty on man to aim at the ideal of non-violence in all he does.

Just as a modern European economist would not consider it a great economic achievement if all European art treasures were sold to America at attractive prices, so the Buddhist economist would insist that a population basing its economic life on non-renewable fuels is living parasitically, on capital instead of income. Such a way of life could have no permanence and could therefore be justified only as a purely temporary expedient. As the world's resources of non-renewable fuels—coal, oil and natural gas—are exceedingly unevenly distributed over the globe and undoubtedly limited in quantity, it is clear that their exploitation at an ever increasing rate is an act of violence against nature which must almost inevitably lead to violence between men.

This fact alone might give food for thought even to those people in Buddhist countries who care nothing for the religious and spiritual values of their heritage and ardently desire to embrace the materialism of modern economics at the fastest possible speed. Before they dismiss Buddhist economics as nothing better than a nostalgic dream, they might wish to consider whether the path of economic development outlined by modern economics is likely to lead them to places where they really want to be. Towards the end of his courageous book *The Challenge of Man's Future,* Professor Harrison Brown of the California Institute of Technology gives the following appraisal:

> "Thus we see that, just as industrial society is fundamentally unstable and subject to reversion to agrarian existence, so within it the conditions which offer individual freedom are unstable in their ability to avoid the conditions which impose rigid organization and totalitarian control. Indeed, when we examine all of the foreseeable difficulties which threaten the survival of industrial civilization, it is difficult to see how the achievement of stability and the maintenance of individual liberty can be made compatible."[8]

Even if this were dismissed as a long-term view—and in the long term, as Keynes said, we are all dead—there is the immediate question of whether 'modernization', as currently practised without regard to religious and spiritual values, is actually producing agreeable results. As far as the masses are concerned, the results appear to be disastrous—a collapse of the rural economy, a rising tide of unemployment in town and country, and the growth of a city proletariat without nourishment for either body or soul.

It is in the light of both immediate experience and long-term prospects that the study of Buddhist economics could be recommended even to those who believe that economic growth is more important than any spiritual or religious values. For it is not a question of choosing between 'modern growth' and 'traditional stagnation'. It is a question of finding the right path of development, the Middle Way between materialist heedlessness and traditionalist immobility, in short, of finding 'Right Livelihood'.

That this can be done is not in doubt. But it requires much more than blind imitation of the materialist way of life of the so-called advanced countries.[9] It requires above all, the conscious and systematic development of a Middle Way in technology, as I have called it,[10, 11] a technology more productive and powerful than the decayed technology of the ancient East, but at the same time non-violent and immensely cheaper and simpler than the labour-saving technology of the modern West.

1. *Pyidawtha, The New Burma.* "Economic and Social Board, Government of the Union of Burma 1954 p. 10.) 2. Ibid., p.8. 3. Ibid., p. 128. 4. Ananda K. Coomaraswamy. *Art and Swadeshi.* Ganesh and Co., Madras, p. 30. 5. J. C. Kumarappa. *Economy of Permanence.* Sarva-Seva-Sangh-Publication, Rajghat, Kashi, 4th ed., 1958, p. 117. 6. J. K. Galbraith. *The Affluent Society.* Penguin, 1962, pp. 272-273. 7. Richard B. Gregg. *A Philosophy of Indian Economic Development.* Navajivan Publishing House, Ahmedabad, 1958, pp. 140-41. 8. Harrison Brown. *The Challenge of Man's Future.* The Viking Press, New York, 1954, p. 255. 9. E. F. Schumacher. 'Rural Industries' in *India at Midpassage.* Overseas Development Institute, London, 1964. 10. E. F. Schumacher. 'Industrialisation through Intermediate Technology' in *Minerals and Industries* Vol. 1, no. 4. Calcutta, 1964. 11. Vijay Chebbi and George McRobie. *Dynamics of District Development.* SIET Institute, Hyderabad 1964.

Vol 1 No 11, Jan-Feb 1968. This article became a chapter in *Small is Beautiful.*

Chapter 4

The New Economics

I WAS BROUGHT UP ON an interpretation of history which suggested that everything started with a few families and then the families got together in tribes; a bit later a lot of tribes joined together into nation states; the nation states became bigger and bigger and formed great regional combinations, 'United States of this', 'United States of that', and finally we could look forward to a single World Government.

Ever since I heard this plausible story I have been observing what is actually happening, and I have seen a proliferation of countries. The United Nations started twenty years ago with about 50 or 60 members, now there are 120 and the number is still growing. In my youth, this was called 'Balkanization' and was thought to be a very bad thing. But what I have been witnessing, over the last 50 years in any case, is a very high degree of Balkanization all over the place, that is to say, large units breaking up into smaller units. Well, it makes you think. Not that everything that happens is necessarily right; but I am sure we should at least notice that it is happening.

Secondly I was brought up on a theory which claimed that in order to be prosperous a country had to be very big, the bigger the better. Look at what Churchill called 'the pumpernickel principalities of Germany', and then look at the Bismarkian Reich: is it not obvious that the great prosperity of Germany only became possible through this combination? All the same, if we make a list of all the most prosperous countries in the world, we find that in overwhelming majority they are very very small; and if you make a list of the largest countries of the world, most of them are exceedingly poor. This again gives one some food for thought.

And thirdly I was brought up on the theory of the economics of scale, that just as with nations so with business and industries, there is an irresistible trend, dictated by modern technology, for the scale of business organisation to become ever bigger. Now, it is

quite true that today there are business organisations that are probably bigger than anything known before in history; but the number
of small units is not declining even in countries like the United
States and many of these small units are extremely prosperous, and
provide society with most of the really fruitful new developments.
So the situation is no doubt a puzzling one for anyone who has
been brought up the way I and most of my age group have been.

We are told, even today, that gigantic organisations are
inescapably necessary, but where they have in fact been created,
what happens? Take General Motors: the great achievement of Mr.
Sloan of General Motors was to structurize this gigantic firm in
such a manner that it became in fact, a federation of firms, none of
them gigantic. And in my own shop, the National Coal Board,
which is the biggest 'firm' in Europe, we are doing something very
similar. Strenuous efforts are being made to structurize it in such a
way that, while remaining one big organisation, it operates and
feels like a federation of what we call 'quasi-firms'. Instead of a
monolith, it becomes a well coordinated assembly of lively,
semi-autonomous units, each with its own drive and sense of
achievement. While many pure theoreticians (who one suspects
may not be very closely in touch with reality) are engaging in the
idolatry of large size, in the actual world there is a tremendous
push and surge to profit from the convenience, humanity and man-
ageability of small size. So much about what anyone can easily
observe for himself.

Let us now approach our subject from another angle and ask
what is *needed*. As in so many other respects, if one looks a bit
more deeply one always finds that at least two things are needed
for human life which appear, on the face of it, to be contradictory.
We need freedom and order: the freedom of lots and lots of small
units and the orderliness of large-scale, possibly global, organisation. When it comes to action, we obviously need small-scale
organisation, because action is a highly personal affair, and one
cannot be in touch with more than a limited number of persons at
any one time. But when it comes to ideology or to ethics, to the
world of ideas, we have to operate in terms of a world-wide unity.
Or to put it differently, it is true that all men are brothers, but it is
also true that when we want to act, in our active personal relations, we can in fact be in touch only with very few of them. And

we all know people who freely talk about the brotherhood of man while treating all their neighbours as enemies—just as we know people who have, in fact, excellent relations with their neighbours, but are at the same time full of the most appalling prejudices about all human groups outside their own particular circle. What I mean to emphasize is our dual requirement: there cannot be a unified solution of all human problems. For his different purposes man needs many different organisations, both small and large ones, both exclusive and comprehensive. Yet people find it most difficult to keep two apparently opposite necessities of truth in their minds at the same time. They always look for a final solution; they insist that it must be a matter of either-or, either you must be in favour of small-scale or in favour of large-scale. It is therefore normally the task of the people who want to do constructive work, not to plug one particular thing, but to restore some kind of balance. The restoration of balance that I believe is needed in our situation today implies a fight against the prevailing idolatry of giantism. (If there were an idolatry in the opposite direction, namely that all large organisations were the work of the devil, then one would have to push in the opposite direction).

The question of scale might be put another way: What is needed in all these matters is to discriminate, to get things sorted out. For every activity there is a certain appropriate scale, and the more active and intimate the activity, the smaller the number of people that can take part, the greater is the number of such relationship arrangements that need to be established. Take teaching: one listens to all sorts of extraordinary debates about the superiority of the University of the Air, or the teaching machine over some other forms of teaching. Well, let us discriminate: What are we trying to teach? It then becomes immediately apparent that certain things can only be taught in a very intimate circle, whereas other things can obviously be taught en masse, via the air, via television, via teaching machines, and so on.

What scale is appropriate? It depends on what we are trying to do. The question of scale is extremely crucial today, in political, social and economic affairs just as in almost everything else. What, for instance, is the appropriate size of a city? And also, one might ask, what is the appropriate size of a country? Now these are serious and difficult questions. It is not possible to programme a computer and get the answer. The really serious matters of life cannot be calculated. We cannot directly calculate what is right, but we jolly well know what is wrong! We can recognize right and wrong at the extremes, although we cannot normally judge them finely enough to say: "This ought to be five per cent more; or that ought to be five per cent less."

Take the question of size of a city. While one cannot judge these things with precision, I think it is fairly safe to say that the upper limit of what is desirable for the size of a city is probably something of the order of half a million. It is quite clear that above such a size nothing is added to the virtue of the city. In places like London, or Tokyo, or New York, the millions do not add to the city's real value but merely create *enormous* problems and produce human degradation. So probably the order of magnitude of five hundred thousand inhabitants could be looked upon as the upper limit. The question of the lower limit of a real city, is much more difficult to judge. The finest cities in history have been very small by 20th Century standards. The instruments and institutions of city culture depend, no doubt, on a certain accumulation of wealth. But how much wealth has to be accumulated depends on the type of culture pursued. Philosophy, the arts and religion cost very very little money. Other types of what claims to be 'high culture', space research or ultra-modern physics cost a lot of money, but are somewhat remote from the real needs of men.

I raise the question of the proper size of cities because, to my mind, this is the most relevant point when we come to consider the most desirable size of nations. I know one cannot draw the map as one sees fit, but it is still legitimate to ask what is the right size of a nation: And this question is closely interrelated with the question of the proper size of cities. Why? This idolatry of giantism that I have talked about is, of course, based on modern technology, particularly as it concerns transport and communications. It has one immensely powerful effect: It makes people *footloose*. Millions of people start moving about, deserting the rural areas and the smaller towns to follow the city lights, to go to the big city, causing a pathological growth. Take the country in which all this is perhaps most exemplified, the United States. Sociologists are studying the problem of 'megalopolis'. The word 'metropolis' is no longer big enough; hence, 'megalopolis'. They freely talk about the polarization

of the population of the United States into three immense megalopolitan areas: one extending from Boston to Washington, a
continuous built-up area, with sixty million people; one around
Chicago, another sixty million; and one on the West Coast, from
San Francisco to San Diego, again a continuous built-up area with
sixty million people, the rest of the country being left practically
empty; deserted provincial towns, and the land cultivated with vast
tractors, combine harvesters, and immense amounts of chemicals.

If this is somebody's conception of the future of the United
States, it is hardly a future worth having. But whether we like it or
not, this is the result of people having become footloose; it is the
result of that marvellous mobility of labour which economists trea-
sure above all else. Let me try an analogy: A large cargo ship can
travel the stormy seas with comparative safety, *provided its load is
secured*; if the load becomes mobile, becomes 'footloose', then the
ship will surely founder. Or let's look at it this way: Everything in
this world has to have a *structure*, otherwise it is chaos. Before we
had mass transport and mass communications, the structure was
simply there, because people were relatively immobile. People who
absolutely wanted to move were in fact amazingly mobile, witness
the great floods of saints from Ireland moving all over Europe.
There were communications; there was mobility; but there was no
footlooseness. The impact of modern technology upon the existing
structure has made it collapse. There is no more structure. A country is like a big cargo ship in which the load is in no way secured:
It tilts one way, and all the load slips that way, and the ship
founders.

One of the chief elements of structure for the whole of mankind
is of course *the state*. And one of the chief elements or instruments
of structuralization (if I may use that term), are *frontiers*, national
frontiers. Now previously, before this technological intervention,
the relevance of frontiers was almost exclusively political and
dynastic; frontiers were delimitations of political power determin-
ing how many people you could raise for war. Economists fought
against such frontiers becoming economic barriers—hence the ideology of free trade. But, then, people and things were not footloose; transport was expensive enough so that movements, both of
people and of goods, were never more than marginal. Trade in the
preindustrial era was not a trade in essentials, but a trade in

precious stones, precious metals, luxury goods, spices. The basic requirements of life had of course to be indigenously produced. And the movement of populations, except in periods of disaster, was confined to persons who had a very special reason to move such as the Irish saints or the scholars of the University of Paris.

But now everything and everybody has become mobile. All structures are threatened, and all structures are vulnerable to an extent that they have never been before. Doctors and psychologists speak of modern society as 'the stress society'. When life is so much easier and the standard of life so much higher than ever before, why should there be a 'stress society'? Because anything that happens, anywhere in the wide wide world, can blow you off course. A business may be sound today; people have learnt it, people have settled down to it—something happens somewhere in the world, and tomorrow it is uneconomic and has to be wiped out. All this, I suggest, is the result of the 'footlooseness' produced by swift and cheap transport and instantaneous communications.

Economics, which Lord Keynes had hoped would settle down as a modest occupation, similar to dentistry, suddenly becomes the most important subject of all. Economic policies absorb almost the entire attention of government, and at the same time become ever more impotent. The simplest things, which only fifty years ago one could see to without difficulty cannot get done any more. The richer a society, the more impossible it becomes to do worth-while things without immediate pay-off. Economics has become such a thralldom that it absorbs almost the whole of foreign policy. People say 'ah yes, we don't like to go with these people, but we depend on them economically so we must humour them.' It tends to absorb the whole of ethics and to take precedence over all other human considerations. Now, quite clearly, this is a pathological development, which has, of course, many roots, but one of its clearly visible roots lies in the great achievements of modern technology in terms of transport and communications.

While people, with an easy-going kind of logic, believe that fast transport and instantaneous communications open up a new dimension of freedom (which they do in some rather trivial respects) they overlook the fact that these achievements also tend to destroy freedom, by making everything extremely vulnerable and extremely insecure, unless—please note—unless conscious policies are developed and conscious action is taken, to mitigate the destructive effects of these technological developments.

Now, these destructive effects are obviously most severe in *large* countries, because, as we have seen, frontiers produce 'structure', and it is a much bigger decision for someone to cross a frontier, to uproot himself from his native land and try and put down roots in another land, than to move within the frontiers of his country. The factor of footlooseness is, therefore, the more serious, the bigger the country. Its destructive effects can be traced both in the rich and in the poor countries. In the rich countries such as the United States of America, it produces, as already mentioned, 'megalopolis'. It also produces a rapidly increasing and ever more intractable problem of 'dropouts', of people who, having become footloose, cannot find a place anywhere in society. Directly connected with this, it produces an appalling problem of crime, alienation, stress, social breakdown, right down to the level of the family. In the poor countries, again most severely in the largest ones, it produces mass migration into cities, mass unemployment, and, as vitality is drained out of the rural areas, the threat of famine. The result is a 'dual society' without any inner cohesion, subject to a maximum of political instability.

As an illustration, let me take the case of Peru. The capital city of Peru, Lima, situated on the Pacific coast, had a population of 175,000 in the early twenties, just over forty years ago. Its population is now approaching three million. The once beautiful Spanish city is now infested by slums, surrounded by misery-belts that are crawling up the Andes. But this is not all. People are arriving from the rural areas at the rate of a thousand a day—and nobody knows what to do with them. The social, or psychological structure of life in the hinterland has collapsed; people have become footloose and arrive in the capital city to squat on some empty land, against the police who come to beat them out, to build their mud hovels and look for a job. *And nobody knows what to do about them.* Nobody knows how to stop the drift.

So, when everybody and everything becomes footloose, the *idea of structure* becomes a really central idea, to which all our powers of thought and imagination must be applied, and, as I said, a primary instrument of structure is the nation state with its frontiers. A large country, I am quite certain, can survive this age of footlooseness only if it achieves a highly articulated *internal* structure, so that in fact it becomes a loose federation of relatively small states, each with its own capital city capable of offering all the culture and facilities which only a city can offer, *including government*. A city without government is obviously second-rate. But how can small countries be 'viable'?

Imagine that in 1864 Bismark had annexed the whole of Denmark instead of only a small part of it, and that nothing had happened since. The Danes would be an ethnic minority in Germany, perhaps struggling to maintain their language by becoming bilingual, the official language of course being German. Only by thoroughly Germanizing themselves could they avoid becoming second-class citizens. There would be an irresistible drift of the most ambitious and enterprising Danes, thoroughly Germanized, to the mainland in the South, and what then would be the status of Copenhagen? That of a remote provincial city. Or imagine Belgium as part of France. What would be the status of Brussels? Again, that of an unimportant provincial city. I don't have to enlarge on it. Imagine now that Denmark a part of Germany, and Belgium a part of France, suddenly turned what is now charmingly called 'nats', wanting independence. There would be endless, heated arguments that these 'non-countries' could not be economically viable, that their desire for independence was, to quote a famous political commentator, 'adolescent emotionalism, political naivety, phoney economics, and sheer bare-faced opportunism'.

How can one talk about the economics of small independent countries? How can one discuss a problem that is a non-problem? There is no such thing as the viability of states or of nations, there is only a problem of viability of people: people, actual persons like you and me, they are viable when they can stand on their own feet and earn their keep. You do not make non-viable people viable by putting large numbers of them into one huge community, and you do not make viable people non-viable by splitting a large community into a number of smaller, more intimate, more coherent and more manageable groups. All this is perfectly obvious and there is absolutely nothing to argue about. Some people ask: "What happens when a country, composed of one rich province and several poor ones falls apart because the rich province secedes?" Most

probably the answer is: "Nothing very much happens." The rich
will continue to be rich and the poor will continue to be poor. "But
if, before secession, the rich province had subsidized the poor, what
happens then?" Well then, of course, the subsidy might stop. But
the rich rarely subsidize the poor; more often they exploit them.
They may not do so directly so much as through the terms of trade.
They may obscure the situation a little by a certain redistribution
of tax revenue or small scale charity, but the last thing they want
to do is secede from the poor.

The normal case is quite different, namely that the poor
provinces wish to separate from the rich, and that the rich want to
hold on because they know that exploitation of the poor within
one's own frontiers is infinitely easier than exploitation of the poor
beyond them. Now if a poor province wishes to secede at the risk
of losing some mythical subsidies, what attitude should one take?

Not that we have to decide this, but what should we think
about it? Is it not a wish to be applauded and respected? Do we
want people to stand on their own feet, as free and self-reliant
men? So again this is a 'non-problem'. I would assert therefore that
there is no problem of viability, as all experience shows. If a country wishes to export all over the world, and import from all over
the world, it has never been held that it had to annex the whole
world in order to do so.

What about the absolute necessity of having a large internal
market? This again is an optical illusion if the meaning of 'large' is
conceived in terms of political boundaries. Needless to say, a prosperous market is better than a poor one, but whether that market
is outside the political boundaries or inside, makes on the whole
very little difference. I am not aware, for instance that Germany, in
order to export a large number of Volkswagens to the United
States, a very prosperous market, could only do so after annexing
the United States. But it does make a lot of difference if a poor
community or province finds itself politically tied to or ruled by a
rich community or province. Why? Because, in a mobile, footloose
society the law of disequilibrium is infinitely stronger than the
so-called law of equilibrium. Nothing succeeds like success, and
nothing stagnates like stagnation. The successful province drains
the life out of the unsuccessful, and without protection against the
strong, the weak have no chance, either they remain weak or they

must migrate and join the strong, they cannot effectively help themselves.

The most important problem in this second half of the twentieth century is the geographical distribution of population, the question of 'regionalism'. But regionalism not in the sense of combining a lot of states into free-trade systems, but in the opposite sense of developing all the regions within each country. This, in fact, is the most important subject on the agenda of all the larger countries today. And a lot of the Nationalism of small nations today, and the desire for self- government and so-called independence, is simply a logical and rational response to the need for regional development. In the poor countries in particular there is no hope for the poor unless there is successful regional development, a development effort outside the capital city covering all the rural areas wherever people happen to be.

If this effort is not brought forth, their only choice is either to remain in their miserable condition where they are, or to migrate into the big city where their condition will be even more miserable. It is a strange phenomenon indeed that the conventional wisdom of present-day economics can do nothing to help the poor.

Invariably it proves that only such policies are viable as have in fact the result of making those already rich and powerful, richer and more powerful. It proves that economic development only pays if it is as near as possible to the capital city or another very large town, and not in the rural areas. It proves that large projects are invariably more economic than small ones, and it proves that capital-intensive projects are invariably to be preferred as against labour-intensive ones. The economic calculus, as applied by present-day economics, forces the industrialist to eliminate the human factor because machines do not make mistakes which people do. Hence the enormous effort at automation and the drive for ever-larger units. This means that those who have nothing to sell but their labour remain in the weakest possible bargaining position. The conventional wisdom of what is now taught as economics bypasses the poor, the very people for whom development is really needed. The economics of giantism and automation are a left over of Nineteenth Century conditions and Nineteenth Century thinking and they are totally incapable of solving any of the real problems of today. An entirely new system of thought is needed, a system based on attention to people, and not primarily attention to goods—(the goods will look after themselves!). It could be summed up in the phrase, 'production by the masses rather than mass production'. What was impossible however in the Nineteenth Century, is possible now. And what was in fact—if not necessarily at least understandable in the Nineteenth Century is unbelievably urgent now. That is, the conscious utilization of our enormous technological and scientific potential for the fight against misery and human degradation; that is a fight in intimate contact with actual people, with individuals, families, small groups, rather than states and other anonymous abstractions. And this presupposes a political and organisational structure that can provide this intimacy.

What is the meaning of democracy, freedom, human dignity, standard of living, self-realization, fulfilment? Is it a matter of goods, or of people? Of course it is a matter of people. But people can be themselves only in small comprehensible groups. Therefore we must learn to think in terms of an articulated structure that can cope with a multiplicity of small-scale units. If economic thinking cannot grasp this it is useless. If it cannot get beyond its vast abstractions, the national income, the rate of growth, capital/output ratio, input-output analysis, labour mobility, capital accumulation, if it cannot get beyond all this and make contact with the human realities of poverty, frustration, alienation, despair, breakdown, crime, escapism, stress, congestion, ugliness and spiritual death, then let us scrap economics and start afresh.

Are there not indeed enough 'signs of the times' to indicate that a new start is needed?

Vol 2 No 3, Sept-Oct 1968

The Critical Question of Size

STATISTICIANS TELL US that the proportion of 'gainfully employed' persons in the service industries is rising while that of industrial workers is falling. This is a development with far-reaching consequences. The production of goods can be, and indeed has been, handed over to machines, and this has led to the so-called growth in productivity which in turn has made possible the growth of incomes. Where do the services stand with regard to the growth of productivity? Can the tendering of services be handed over to machines? ' The answer is an absolute No. If the human factor is taken out of the service, the service disappears and its place may or may not be taken by a labour-saving device. People's need to render service to their fellows cannot be satisfied if machines take their place. The human element disappears.

Of course, it cannot disappear altogether, and where actual people continue to render actual services—teachers, nurses and countless others—increases in productivity cannot be generally obtained, because they mainly depend on machines, not on people. To the extent that advances in wages are made dependent on advances in productivity the service industries tend to fall behind. But the people in service industries, not surprisingly, insist on keeping in step with the others. As a result, the service industries costs rise very much faster than those of other industries, and the pressure on them to 'rationalise' increases. But how call you rationalise services? Only by reducing the human element, by substituting machines, or by reducing the service. The drive for higher productivity and lower costs in the service industries therefore almost inevitably results in a further elimination of the human factor.

If my description is correct, it follows that our need to render service to our fellows is becoming more and more difficult to satisfy. The difficulty is compounded as the size of service organisations increases and as, in the pursuit of efficiency, they become more centralised and more 'scientifically' organised.

This has many reasons, which have been more or less systematically identified by sociologists, systems analysis, and others. But you do not have to be an expert in sociology or systems analysis to be able to see that the human factor, as a person-to-person relationship, depends on a certain degree of intimacy, which no-one can achieve with large numbers of people. How many people do we get to know as people in the course of a lifetime? If we made a list of them we should find the number surprisingly small—perhaps a few hundred, certainly not a few thousand. If I work inside a group of people, I need to know not only how I get on with each of them; I also need to know how each of them gets on with, and relates to, everyone else. The number of person-to-person relationships within a group rises much faster than the number of group members as the group increases in size. Among three people, there are three bilateral relationships; among twelve, there are sixty-six; among a hundred, there are 4,950—more than anyone call keep in his head at the same time. In fact any large group or people will inevitably break down into small groups, whether such a breakdown is provided for in the organisation chart or not. Structures will emerge, and such structures are normally hierarchical, that is to say. there are a number of 'levels' between the top and the bottom. Everybody has a boss; the little bosses have bigger bosses and so on, if not 'ad infinitum', in general through quite a few layers of authority: the bigger the organisation, the more such layers there are likely to be.

Such structures cannot function without many rules and regulations which everybody, even the top boss, has to abide by. It follows that nobody, not even the top boss, can act freely, though at each level there may of course be a certain amount of discretion.

One of our fundamental needs is to be able to act in accordance with our moral impulses. In a big organisation our freedom to do so is inevitably severely restricted. Our primary duty is to stay within the rules and regulations, which, although contrived by human beings, are not themselves human beings. No matter how carefully drawn up, they lack the flexibility of the 'human touch'.

The bigger the organisation, the less is it possible for any member of it to act freely as a moral being; the more frequent are the occasions when someone will say: "I am sorry. I know what I am doing is not quite right, but these are my instructions" or "these are the regulations I am paid to implement" or "I myself agree with you; perhaps you could take the matter to a higher level, or to your member of parliament."

As a result, big organisations often behave very badly, very immorally, very stupidly and inhumanely, not because the people inside them are any of these things but simply because the organisation carries the load of bigness. The people inside them are then criticised by people outside, and such criticism is of course justified and necessary, but it bears the wrong address. It is not the people of the organisation but its size that is at fault. It is like blaming a car's exhaust gases on the driver; even an angel could not drive a car without fouling the air.

This is a situation of universal frustration: the people inside the organisation are morally frustrated because they lack freedom of action, and the people outside are frustrated because, rare exceptions apart, their legitimate moral complaints find no positive response and all too often merely produce evasive, meaningless, blandly arrogant, or downright offensive replies.

Many books have been written about moral individuals in immoral society. As society is composed of individuals, how could a society be more immoral than its members? It becomes immoral if its structure is such that moral individuals cannot act in accordance with their moral impulses. And one method of achieving this dreadful result is by letting organisations become too large. (I am not asserting that there are no evil individuals capable of doing evil things no matter what may be the size of organisations or, generally, the structure of society. It is when ordinary, decent, harmless people do evil things that society gets into the deepest troubles.)

There are three things healthy people most need to do—to be creatively productive, to render service, and to act in accordance with their moral impulses. In all three respects modern society frustrates most of the people most of the time. Frustration makes people unhappy and often unhealthy. It can make them violent or completely listless. It makes them feel insignificant and powerless. As a sensitive British worker put it:

> "The factory I work in is part of one of those combines which seem to have an ambition to become the great provider, both in and out of work, for their employees. Recreational facilities

abound; but the number of people using them is small in percentage. Perhaps others, like me, resent the gradual envelopment of recreation by the umbrella of factory life. Not only recreation either. The firm has a mania to appear responsible. Fingers of charity stretch ever further into communal life. The company bends over backwards to make amends for the lethargy that the factory has produced in the worker. The effect is treated while the cause is ignored. No wonder the worker is unappreciative."

"The alienating conditions of modern work," says C. Wright Mills, "now include the salaried employees as well as the wage-workers. There are few, if any, features of wage-work. . . that do not characterise at least some white-collar work." And David Jenkins in his recent book on *Job Power* comments: "White-collar and service work environments have been steadily degraded, with the growth of importance of these sectors and the refinement of management techniques, developed primarily for use in manufacturing, applied to other types of work. . . As a result of the refinements of dehumanising management techniques, white-collar workers have been rapidly catching up with blue-collar workers in terms of alienation."

Alienation, frustration, boredom, brutalisation, resentment, lack of appreciation. . . the greatest single failure of the modern scheme of things is what it has made of work. Anyone who can say, honestly and convincingly, "I enjoy my work", has become an object of astonishment and envy. Work, as the sociologists say, has become purely instrumental; unlike sport, it is not being undertaken for the joy of it, since for most people the joy his gone out of it; it is undertaken as a hateful necessity because people have to make a living. Those who can get a living without doing work are being envied even more intensely than those who enjoy, actually enjoy, their work. This is where modern society has snookered itself. Its masters call upon the people to work harder, to do a fair day's work for a fair day's pay; but for most of them 'a fair day's work' has become a contradiction in terms.

The people's power derives from their power to work, to work creatively, to render service, to act in accordance with their moral impulses. Joyless, meaningless, 'alienated' work has no power. Let me again quote a British worker:

"It is probably wrong to expect factories to be other than they are. After all, they are built to house machines, not people. Inside a factory it soon becomes obvious that steel brought to life by electricity takes precedence over flesh and blood. The onus is on the machines to such an extent that they appear to assume human attributes of those who work them. Machines have become as much like people as people have become like machines. . . They pulsate with life, while human beings become robots. Too many people are imprisoned in organisations which, on account of their superhuman size, make people insignificant and powerless."

If this is so—to the extent that this is so—people's power is frustrated and paralysed. Neither the further development of this type of mechanisation nor the streamlining and perfection of this type of organisation can restore people's power and lead us out of our predicament. Decent survival now depends on redesigning technology and redesigning organisations.

It strikes me as astonishing how little systematic study has been given to the all-pervading question of size. Aristotle knew about its importance, and so did Karl Marx who insisted that with changes in quantity you get, at certain thresholds, changes in quality. Aristotle said: "To the size of states there is a limit, as there is to other things, plants, animals, implements; for none of these retain their natural power when they are too large or too small, but they either wholly lose their nature or are spoiled."

Organisations, like these 'other things', may well grow to such a size that they wholly lose their nature or are altogether spoiled. An organisation may have been set up to render various services to all sorts of helpless, needy people; it grows and grows, and suddenly you find that it does not serve the people any more but simply pushes them around. There may be complaints that the organisation has become 'too bureaucratic' and there may be denunciations of the bureaucrats. There may be demands that the 'incompetent bosses' of the organisation be replaced by better people. But few people seem to realise that bureaucracy is a necessary and unavoidable concomitant of excessive size; that bureaucrats cannot help being bureaucratic; and that the apparent incompetence of the bosses has almost nothing to do with their personal competence.

A large organisation, to be able to function at all, requires an elaborate administrative structure. Administration is a most difficult and exacting job which call be done only by exceptionally industrious people. The administrators of a large organisation cannot deal concretely with real-life problems and situations: they have to deal with them abstractly. They cannot enjoy themselves by devising, as it were, the perfect shoe for a real foot: their task is to devise composite shoes to fit all possible feet. The variety of real life is inexhaustible, and they cannot make a special rule for every individual case. Their task is to anticipate all possible cases and to frame a minimum number of rules—a small minimum indeed!—to fit them all. We all know that life, all too often, is stranger than fiction: the dilemma of the administrators, therefore, is severe: either they make innumerable rules, the enforcement of which then requires whole armies of minor officials, or they limit themselves to a few rules which then produce innumerable hard cases and absurdities calling for special treatment; every special treatment, however, constitutes a precedent which is, in effect, a new rule.

The organisation as a whole, at the same time, is faced with a further dilemma: either it draws its best brains into the administration whereupon they may be missed at operational level; or it uses its best talents at operational level, whereupon there may be serious frustration down below, owing to incompetent administration.

If there is any truth in this (very rough) analysis, the conclusion is obvious: let us organise units of such a size that their administrative requirements become minimal. In other words, let us have them on a *human* scale, so that the need for rules and regulations is minimised and all difficult cases can be resolved, as it were, on the spot, face to face, without creating precedents—for where there is no rule there cannot be a precedent.

The problem of administration is thus reduced to a problem of size. Small units are self-administrating in the sense that they do not require full-time administrators of exceptional ability; almost anybody can see to it that things are kept in reasonable order and everything that needs to be done is done by the right person at the right time.

I should add that, as Aristotle observed, things must be neither too big nor too small. I have no doubt that for every organisation, as for other things, there is a 'critical size' which must be attained before the organisation can have any effectiveness at all. But this is hardly a thought that needs to be specially emphasised, since everybody understands it instinctively. What does need to be emphasised is that 'critical size' is likely to be very much smaller than most people in our mass society are inclined to believe.

Excessive size not only produces the dilemma of administration, it also makes many problems virtually insoluble. To illustrate what I mean, imagine an island of 2,000 inhabitants—I have in mind an island of this size which a little while ago demanded total sovereignty and independence. Crime on such an island is a rarity; maybe there is one single full-time policeman, maybe there is none. Assume, however, that some crimes do occur, that some people are sent to jail, and that they return from jail at the rate of one person a year. There is no difficulty in re-integrating this one ex-prisoner into the island's society. Some-one, somewhere will find this person a room to live in and some kind of work. No problem.

The British Isles contain not 2,000 but 50 million inhabitants, and the number of people returning from prison every year is about 25,000. Arithmetic teaches us that

$$2,000 : 1 = 50 \text{ million} : 25,000.$$

But it is not true. Marx was more realistic than is dreamt of in arithmetic when he said that a change in quantity produces a change in quality. The problem of re-integrating 25,000 ex-prisoners into a society 25,000 times as large as that of a little island is quite a different problem, not only quantitatively but also qualitatively, a problem the solution of which escapes the devoted efforts of Home Office, Probation Service, and countless other organisations. Is it a matter of proportionately too little effort and money being devoted to this task of reintegration and rehabilitation? Could we solve the problem by having bigger prisoners' aid organisations, more people, and more money? Maybe we can; maybe we cannot. I personally think we cannot. But the point is that the small island does not have this problem. The engine, as it were, is small enough to consume its own smoke. Or we might say: *People's power prevents the problem from becoming a problem.* Not merely does it prevent crime from becoming a problem, it also prevents the consequences of crime from becoming a problem.

This, surely, is a matter of breathtaking importance. People's power doesn't solve problems: it avoids them. Of course, some work is needed to avoid problems; but this is the kind of work which people want to do. They want to do it because, to become real, they need to do it. They need to follow their moral impulses; they need to render service to their fellows, and they need to be creatively productive. So, when we need something, we do not expect to be paid for it. On the contrary, there are countless people who say: "This is what I want to do; I don't expect payment for it, I don't even want my expenses back: it is what I want to do."

The question is: How can people's power be 'liberated'? By going for the small, the human, scale. I do not wish to be dogmatic on this because I do not know how to define what, in any particular instance, is the 'human scale'. When many people are doing exactly the same thing—as for instance in a large orchestra with twenty first violinists and twenty second violinists, etc.—the proper scale, expressed in numbers of people, will undoubtedly be different from that of a team in which everybody is doing something different from everybody else. So there is no easy, generalised answer. It is, as they say, 'Horses for courses'. But it *is* horses for courses; it is not the bigger the better, which is the all too common assumption of the modern world.

Whether in a governmental or voluntary, non-governmental organisation, the human touch and the mobilisation of people's power remain wishful thinking unless the organisation is of the right size, both geographically and numerically. 'Right size' is a difficult concept: the touchstone is the reaction of people—can they still give or receive individual attention? My own guess is that we should accustom ourselves to thinking in terms of very much smaller units than we may be inclined to, conditioned as we are by a society addicted to 'rationalisation by giantism'. On a small scale people's power can be mobilised but when the scale becomes too large, people's power becomes frustrated and ineffective. What, precisely, is the right scale, I cannot say. We should experiment to find out. I could imagine an arrangement whereby in this country, say, 20-25 units would be constituted, with an average of something like 2-2.5 million people each. All but a small percentage of the taxes raised in these units would be returned to them, to use as they saw fit. They would be the masters of their own fate, as if they were separate countries, and that there was no central 'government' to bail them out if they made a mess of things. The engagement of people's power, may then become a phenomenon all over Britain. I have seen this happening in some parts of the world, for instance in China, but also in communities under entirely different systems. The discovery and mobilisation of people's power may be nothing less than the condition of survival for the hitherto affluent societies of the West.

Vol 6 No 3, July-Aug 1975

WORK & LEISURE

Chapter 6

Insane Work Cannot Produce A Sane Society

"Dante, when composing his visions of hell, might well have included the mindless, repetitive boredom of working on a factory assembly line. It destroys initiative and rots brains, yet millions of British workers are committed to it for most of their lives."

THE REMARKABLE THING IS THAT the above statement in *The Times*, like countless similar ones made before it, aroused no interest: there were no hot denials or anguished agreements; no reactions at all. The strong and terrible words—visions of hell—mindless, repetitive boredom—destroying initiative and rotting brains— millions of British workers, committed for most of their lives— attracted no reprimand that they were misstatements or over-statements, that they were irresponsible or hysterical exagger- ations or subversive propaganda; no, people read them, sighed and nodded, I suppose, and moved on.

Not even the ecologists, the conservationists, the doom-watchers and warners are interested in this matter. If someone had asserted that certain man-made arrangements had destroyed the initiative and rotted the brains of millions of birds, or seals, or wild animals in the game reserves of Africa, such an assertion would have been either refuted or taken as a serious challenge. If someone had asserted that not the minds or souls or brains of millions of British workers were being 'rotted' but their bodies, there would have been considerable interest; after all, there are safety regulations, inspectorates, claims for damages, and so forth. No management is unaware of its duty to avoid accidents or physical conditions which impair workers' health. But workers' brains, minds and souls are a different matter.

A semi-official report, published by Her Majesty's Stationery Office, bears the title 'Pollution: Nuisance or Nemesis'. It contains no reference to man-made arrangements which destroy the initiative and rot the brains of millions of workers. Nor, indeed, would any reader even expect such references. He expects and finds learned discussions of 'Some harmful pollutants'—DDT and PCB, metals, phosphates and nitrates, sulphur dioxide, etc.—and warnings of the modern perils—cancers, birth defects and mutations, that is all. He may fully share the authors' concluding hope, when they say: "We hope that society will be educated and informed. . . so that pollution may be brought under control and mankind's population and consumption of resources be steered towards a permanent and sustainable equilibrium. Unless this is done (they continue) sooner or later—and some believe there is little time left—the downfall of civilisation will not be a matter of science fiction. It will be the experience of our children and grandchildren."

But it would hardly occur to him—the average reader—that the destruction of initiative and the rotting of brains of millions of workers could be classed as the worst pollution of all, the greatest peril, and the most important danger for something to be done about to avoid the 'downfall of civilisation'.

If it is thought that it may be a bit far-fetched to deal with the rotting of brains under the heading of pollution, it will perhaps not be considered unreasonable to look for a treatment of this subject under the heading of 'Natural Resources: Sinews for Survival' which is the title of a companion volume, also published by Her Majesty's Stationery Office. The most important of all resources is obviously the initiative, imagination and brain power of man himself. We all know this and are ready to devote very substantial funds to what we call education. So, if the problem is survival, one might fairly expect to find some discussion relating to the preservation and, if possible, the development of the most precious of all natural resources, human brains. However, such expectations are not fulfilled. 'Sinews for Survival' deals with all the natural factors—minerals, energy, water, wildlife and so forth—but not at all with such immaterial resources as initiative, intelligence and brainpower.

Similarly, I might refer to the international report on *The Limits to Growth* prepared for The Club of Rome's project on the predicament of mankind. This report has caused a world-wide stir because it purports to demonstrate, with the help of a computerized world-model, that growth along the established lines cannot now continue for long without leading to inescapable breakdown. The authors therefore plead for policies which would lead to "a desirable, sustainable state of global equilibrium". They believe that "much more information is needed to manage the transition to global equilibrium. . . The most glaring deficiencies in present knowledge occur in the pollution sector of the model. . . How long does it take for a given pollutant to travel from its point of release to its point of entrance into the human body?" (p.180).

There is, here again, no reference to pollutants entering the human mind or soul. But the report does say this: "The final, most elusive and most important information we need deals with human values. As soon as society recognises that it cannot maximize everything for everyone, it must begin to make choices. Should there be more people or more wealth, more wilderness or more automobiles, more food for the poor or more services for the rich?" (p.181). We might say: what a collection of choices! Even in connection with 'human values' a choice affecting the rotting of human minds or brains finds no mention. And this is yet another example of the lack of interest in the vital question of *human work and what the work does to the worker*.

Considering the centrality of work in human life, one might have expected that every textbook on economics, sociology, politics and related subjects would present a theory of work as one of the indispensable foundation stones for all further expositions. After all, it is work which occupies most of the energies of the human race, and what people actually *do* is normally more important, for understanding them, than what they say, or what they spend their money on, or what they own, or how they vote. A person's work is unquestionably one of the most formative influences on his character and personality.

However, the truth of the matter is that we look in vain for such presentations of theories of work in these textbooks. The question of what the work does to the worker is hardly ever asked, not to mention the question of whether the real task might not be to adapt the work to the needs of the worker rather that demanding of the worker to adapt himself to the needs of the work—which means, of course, primarily: to the needs of the machine.

It is not as if there were any lack of studies and reports on productivity, on workers' morale, workers' participation in management, and so forth. But they do not seem to germinate any fundamentally new thinking: they do not raise questions about the validity or sanity of a system which destroys men's initiative and rots their brains. They all—although in varying degree—start from the implicit assumption that the *kind* or *quality* of work to be done in society is simply what it is: somebody has to do it; if it is soul-destroying work, that is regrettable but unalterable. If people do not like doing it, we pay them more and more until enough people like the money more than they dislike the work. But, of course, this economic solution of the problem—paying what the law of supply and demand prescribes—is no solution from our point of view; some people, as St. Augustine observed, even take pleasure in deformities, and many are prepared—or they are forced—to ruin themselves for money. We are concerned with the fact that our *system* of production, in many of its parts, is such that it destroys men's initiative and rots their brains, and inflicts this damage not on a few people by way of exception, but on millions of them by way of everyday routine. Why men or women tolerate it and accept it against pecuniary compensation is quite a different question.

We may remind ourselves of the teaching of the Church in this connection. "No man," said Pope Leo XIII (R.N.32-3), "may with impunity outrage that human dignity which God Himself treats with great reverence, nor stand in the way of that higher life which is the preparation for the eternal life of heaven. Nay, more: no man has in this matter power over himself. To consent to any treatment which is calculated to defeat the end and purpose of his being is beyond his right; he cannot give up his soul to servitude, for it is not man's own rights which are here in question, but the rights of God, the most sacred and inviolable of rights."

Let us ask then: How does work relate to the end and purpose of man's being? It has been universally recognised, in all authentic teachings of mankind, that every being born into this world has to work not merely to keep himself alive but to strive towards perfection. "Be ye therefore perfect, even as your Father which is in heaven is perfect." To keep himself alive, he needs various goods and services, which will not be forthcoming without labour. To perfect himself, he needs purposeful activity in accordance with the injunction, "Whichever gift each of you may have received, use it in service to one another, like good stewards dispensing the grace of God in its varied forms." (1 Peter, 4:10).

From this, we may derive the three purposes of human work as follows:

First: to provide society with the goods and services which are necessary or useful to it,
Second: to enable every one of us to use and thereby perfect our gifts like good stewards; and
Third: to do so in service to, and in co-operation with, others, so as to liberate ourselves from our in-born egocentricity.

This three-fold function makes work so central to human life that it is truly impossible to conceive of life at the human level without work, which the Church declares, "even after original sin, was decreed by Providence for the good of man's body and soul".

The kind and quality of work to be done is implicitly taken as given; somebody has to do it whether we like it or not. The time has come to question this implicit assumption and to attack this immobilism. Mindless work is as intolerable in a society that wishes to be sane and civilised as filthy air or stinking water, nay, it is even more intolerable. Why can't we set new tasks to our scientists and engineers, our chemists and technologists, many of whom are becoming increasingly doubtful about the *human relevance* of their own work? Has the affluent society nothing to spare for anything really new? Is 'bigger, faster, richer' still the only line of development we can conceive, when we know that it entails the perversion of human work so that, as one of the Popes put it, "from the factory dead matter goes out improved, whereas men there are corrupted and degraded"? . . .and that it also entails environmental degradation and the speedy exhaustion of the earth's non-renewable resources. Could we not devote at least a fraction of our research and development (R & D) efforts to create what might be called a technology with a human face?

This 'human face' would reflect, to start with,, in a certain way, the size of the human being: in other words, we should explore whether at least some organisations and some machines could not be made small enough to suit the human scale. Countless people long for a chance to become their own masters, independent and self-reliant—which they cannot become unless it is possible to be efficient on a small scale. Where is the small scale equipment, where are the mini-plants to give a chance to the small man who can and wants to stand on his own feet?

People say: it can't be done: small scale is uneconomic. How do they know? While the idea that 'bigger is better' may have been a 19th century truth, now, owing to the advance of knowledge and technical ability, it has become—not all along the line, but over wide fields of application—a twentieth century myth.

I have in mind, as an example, a production unit developed by the Intermediate Technology Development Group which costs around £5000. The smallest unit previously available cost £250,000, fifty times as much, and had a capacity about 50 times as great. The makers of this large-scale unit were completely convinced that any smaller unit would be hopelessly uneconomic. But they were wrong. Think of it: instead of one unit requiring for its efficient operation a vast and complicated organisation, we can now have fifty units, each of them 'on the human scale', each of them large enough for a few enterprising people to make an honest living, but none of them so large as to make anyone inordinately rich. Think of the simplification of transport if there can be many small units instead of one large one, each of them drawing on local raw materials and working for nearby local markets. Think of the social and individual human consequences of such a change of scale.

Admittedly, this kind of work was initially undertaken solely with a view to helping the developing countries where on account of poverty markets are small, unemployment is high, capital is scarce, and transport is generally difficult and expensive. But it became quickly apparent that the results of this work were of equal interest to many communities in the over-developed countries, because everywhere there are innumerable people who are excluded from the productive process in a validly human sense because organisations, capital requirements and machines have become so big that only people already very rich and powerful can get hold of them and all the others can merely be what might be called 'technological gap-fillers'.

A technology with a human face would not only favour smallness as against the current giantism; it would also favour simplicity as against complexity. It is, of course, much more difficult to make things relatively simple again than to make them ever more complicated. I am not talking about the simple life as such—although there is much to be said in its favour: I am talking about processes of production, distribution and exchange, as well as about the design of products. Complexity, in itself often the result of excessive size and the excessive elimination of the human factor, demands a degree of specialisation and division of labour which all-too-often kills the human content of work and makes people too specialised to be able to attain wisdom. It must therefore be seen as an evil, and it is the task of human intelligence—of R & D in the industrial context—to minimise this evil, not to let it proliferate.

All this, I believe, hangs together. All is related to the human scale, all related to the humanisation of human work, all conducive to the re-integration of the human being into the productive process, so that he or she can feel alive, creative, happy in short, a real person—even while they are working for their living.

If one thing stares us in the face, it is that insane work cannot produce a sane society. There is no reason to believe that today, with so much knowledge, so brilliant a science, and such astounding technological skills at our disposal, we should be incapable of extending the joy of creative productive work to those millions of people who are at present deprived of it. A sane society cannot emerge if, is Paul Goodman called it, millions of youngsters are 'growing up absurd'; or if millions of men and women are condemned, most of their lives, to do work which destroys their initiative and rots their brains; or, indeed, if all—or most of—useful, productive, creative work is handed over to machines controlled by giant corporations, while people—real living people—are told to find their fulfilment in leisure activities.

Vol 5 No 2, May-June 1974

Public Funds for Voluntary Work

WORLD BANK AND OTHER STATISTICS purport to show that there are many hundreds of millions of people in the world today who have an annual income of less than $100. The most important question raised by such information is this: "How do they manage to stay alive?"

I don't think I know anybody in Europe who could survive on $2 or less a week; yet, if the statistics are to be believed, many hundreds of millions of people are actually doing so. They must possess a knowledge or capability altogether unknown to us. This knowledge or capability, no doubt, expresses itself in their 'life-style' or 'pattern of living' which, however unsatisfactory it may appear from a rich man's point of view, has an uncanny and incredible survival power. If it did not have this power, all these people would be dead; but, as has often been remarked, poor people don't die of poverty. They have a survival ability which better-off people normally lack.

If 'development' weakens or destroys this survival ability, it is a killer disease: incomes may rise from, say, $100 per person per year to $150 or even $200; yet misery deepens and turns into despair. The appropriateness of the 'pattern of living' is of immensely greater importance than the amount of income disclosed by statistics. These things are difficult to grasp; but if those who are pursuing development fail to take account of them, they are likely to do more harm than good.

A crudely materialistic philosophy induces policy makers to think of goods before they think of people. They look at a group of people and say: "These people lack consumer goods. So let us make arrangements for the production of such goods on an adequate scale." What is wrong with this approach ? Obviously, the output of consumer goods is intended to benefit the people. But will it?

Instead of saying: "These people lack consumer goods", one

might say: "These people lack the ability to make consumer goods. So let us try and help them to acquire the relevant ability or abilities."

This approach would try to build on what is already there, instead of pushing existing patterns out of the way and attempting to substitute quite different ones. It would be based on the motto: "Let's study what they are doing and see if we can help them to do it better."

It is not possible to help the poor to help themselves, except by first learning from the poor—learning the secrets of their arts of survival. To assume the attitude of a learner requires a degree of genuine humility and respect which is not easily attained by people who have been conditioned to think of poor peasants as backward and inferior to educated townsmen.

Humility and respect—these are high human qualities which, generally speaking, do not tend to flourish in large, bureaucratic institutions, particularly when these are backed by State power. Powerful civil servants tend to be more conscious of their power than of their status of servants or their duty of civility. In short, they tend to be poor learners.

This is where the Voluntary Agencies are of immense value. They tend to have virtually no power; they can offer no security of tenure to their staffs. Hence they tend to attract people imbued with a genuine desire to serve their fellow men and not to lord it over them.

The government machine is generally very efficient in raising money and relatively inefficient in spending it. Voluntary Agencies, on the other hand, have many people genuinely anxious to serve, which means that they are very efficient in spending money; but they have great trouble in raising it.

This seems to be an ideal situation for some kind of active *symbiosis:* let the government raise the money and let the Voluntary Agencies spend it.

Whose money is it anyhow? It is money earned by the public at large; some of it is needed for 'development'; it needs to be 'raised' and 'spent'. The only question is: "Who is most competent in spending it?" I hold that the answer is perfectly obvious.

Any astute government, whether aid-giving or aid-receiving, would therefore most assiduously study the possibilities of achieving this *symbiosis*. Needless to say, when public funds are to be disbursed by private Voluntary Agencies, there has to be *accountability*.

Now, the art of *accountability* has been perfected and is being practised with a high degree of skill—by whom? By large-scale business, e.g. multi-national corporations.

You may say that many multi-national corporations often do not, in fact, behave very well. It is not their system of control but their policy that is at fault in such cases. What can be learned from them is how to exercise *accountability* without unduly impairing the freedom of action of the lower formations, i.e. the 'people in the field'. This is an art—or a technique—that has been mastered by the large-scale businesses, and it can be learned. If there is proper *accountability*, the way is open for the supply of public funds to private Voluntary Agencies; and this would make real development work infinitely more effective and more 'made to measure' than it ever has been in the past.

The new Government in India is said to be of 'Gandhian' complexion. An essential element of Gandhianism is the insistence that development must come mainly 'from below', from the villages, and not 'from above', from the Central or State Government. I think this is right. But what does it mean in practice? Is government to sit back and wait for initiatives from the villages? Maybe the villages that most need development are so run down that no real initiatives can be expected to come from them. The initiatives themselves have to be initiated. This can be done only by private Voluntary Agencies which operate without power.

As long as these Agencies have to spend their best intelligence and effort on raising money—and can never raise enough—their effectiveness is simply inadequate. So the answer seems to me to be obvious: private effort supported by public funds.

Vol 8 No 4, Sept-Oct 1977

Conscious Culture of Poverty

Schon in der Kindheit hört' ich es mit Beben:
Nur wer im Wohlstand lebt, lebt angenehm.
Berthold Brecht[1]

ONLY THE RICH can have a good life—this is the daunting message that has been drummed into the ears of all humankind during the last half-century or so. It is the implicit doctrine of 'development'; the growth of income serves as the very criterion of progress. Everyone, it is held, has not only the right but the duty to become rich, and this applies to societies even more than individuals. The most succinct and most relevant indicator of a country's status in the world is thought to be *average income per head*, while the prime object of admiration is not the level already attained but the current rate of growth.

It follows logically—or so it seems—that the greatest obstacle to progress is a growth of population: it frustrates, diminishes, off-sets what the growth of Gross National Product (GNP) would otherwise achieve. What is the point of, let us say, doubling GNP over a period if population is also allowed to double during the same time? It would mean running fast merely to stand still: *average income per head* would remain stationary, and there would be no advance at all towards the cherished goal of universal affluence.

In the light of this received doctrine, the well-nigh unanimous prediction of the demographers—that world population, barring unforeseen catastrophes, will double during the next thirty years—is taken as an intolerable threat. What other prospect is this than one of limitless frustration?

Some mathematical enthusiasts are still content to project the economic 'growth curves' of the last thirty years for another thirty or even fifty years, to 'prove' that all humankind can become immensely rich within a generation or two. Our only danger, they suggest, is to succumb, at this glorious hour in the history of progress, to a 'failure of nerve'. They presuppose the existence of limitless resources in a finite world; an equally limitless capacity of living nature to cope with pollution; and the omnipotence of science and social engineering.

The sooner we stop living in the cloud-cuckoo-land of such fanciful projections and presuppositions the better it will be, and this applies to the people of the rich countries just as much as to those of the poor. *It would apply even if all population growth stopped entirely forthwith.*

The modern assumption that 'only the rich can have a good life' springs from a crudely materialistic philosophy which contradicts the universal tradition of humankind. The material *needs* of human beings are limited and in fact quite modest, even though our material *wants* may know no bounds. We do not live by bread alone, and no increase in our *wants* can give us 'the good life'.

To make my meaning clear, let me state right away that there are degrees of poverty which may be totally inimical to any kind of culture in the ordinarily accepted sense. They are essentially different from 'poverty' and deserve a separate name; the term that offers itself is '*misery*'. We may say that poverty prevails when people have enough to keep body and soul together but little to spare, whereas in misery they cannot keep body and soul together, and even the soul suffers deprivation. Some thirteen years ago, when I began seriously to grope for answers to these perplexing questions, I wrote this in *Roots of Economic Growth*.[2]

> "All peoples—with exceptions that merely prove the rule—have always known how to help themselves, they have always *discovered a pattern of living which fitted their peculiar natural surroundings*. Societies and cultures have collapsed when they deserted their own pattern and fell into decadence, but even then, unless devastated by war, the people normally continued to provide for themselves, with something to spare for higher things. Why not now, in so many parts of the world? I am not speaking of ordinary poverty, but of actual and acute misery; not of the poor, who according to the universal tradition of mankind are in a special way blessed, but of the miserable and degraded ones who, by the same tradition, should not exist at all and should be helped by all. Poverty may have been the rule

in the past, but misery not. Poor peasants and artisans have existed from time immemorial; but miserable and destitute villagers in their thousands and urban pavement dwellers in their hundreds of thousands—not in wartime or as an aftermath of war, but in the midst of peace and as a seemingly permanent feature—that is a monstrous and scandalous thing which is altogether abnormal in the history of mankind. We cannot be satisfied with the snap answer that this is due to population pressure.

Since every mouth that comes into the world is also endowed with a pair of hands, population pressure could serve as an explanation only if it meant an absolute shortage of land—and although that situation may arise in the future, it decidedly has not arrived today (a few islands excepted). It cannot be argued that population increase as such must produce increasing poverty because the additional pairs of hands could not be endowed with the capital they needed to help themselves. Millions of people have started without capital and have shown that a pair of hands can provide not only the income but also the durable goods, i.e. capital, for civilised existence. So the question stands and demands an answer. What has gone wrong? Why cannot these people help themselves?"

The answer, I suggest, lies in the abandonment of their indigenous 'culture of poverty', which means not only that they lost true culture but also that their poverty, in too many cases, has turned into misery.

A culture of poverty as we have known in innumerable variants before the industrial age is based on one fundamental distinction—which may have been made consciously or instinctively, it does not matter—the distinction between the 'ephemeral' and the 'eternal'. All religions, of course, deal with this distinction, suggesting that the ephemeral is relatively unreal and only the eternal is real. On the material plane we deal with goods and services, and the same distinction applies: all goods and services can be arranged, as it were, on a scale which extends from the ephemeral to the eternal. Needless to say, neither of these terms may be taken in an absolute sense (because there is nothing absolute on the material plane), although there may well be something absolute in the maker's *intention*: he/she may see his/her product as something to be used up, that is to say, to be destroyed in the act of consumption; or as something to be used or enjoyed as a permanent asset, ideally for ever.

The extremes are easily recognised. An article of consumption, like a loaf of bread, is *intended* to be *used up*; while a work of art, like the Mona Lisa, is *intended* to be there for ever. Transport services to take a tourist on holiday are intended to be used up and therefore ephemeral; while a bridge across the river is intended to be a permanent facility. Entertainment is intended to be ephemeral; while education (in the fullest sense) is intended to be eternal.

Between the extremes of the ephemeral and the eternal, there extends a vast range of goods and services with regard to which the producer may exercise a certain degree of choice: he/she may be producing with the intention of supplying something relatively ephemeral or something relatively eternal. A publisher, for instance, may produce a book with the intention that it should be purchased, read, and treasured by countless generations; or the intention may be that it should be purchased, read, and thrown away as quickly as possible.

Ephemeral goods are—to use the language of business—'depreciating assets' and have to be 'written off'. Eternal goods, on the other hand, are never 'depreciated' but 'maintained'. (You don't depreciate the Taj Mahal: you try to maintain its splendour for all time.)

Ephemeral goods are subject to the economic calculus. Their only value lies in being used up, and it is necessary to ensure that their cost of production does not exceed the benefit derived from destroying them. But eternal goods are not intended for destruction; so there is no occasion for an economic calculus, because the benefit—the product of annual value and time—is infinite and therefore incalculable.

Once we recognise the validity of the distinction between the ephemeral and the eternal, we are able to distinguish, in principle, between two different types of 'standard of living'. Two societies may have the same volume of production and the same *income per head of population*, but the *quality of life* or life-style may show fundamental and incomparable differences; the one placing its main emphasis on ephemeral satisfactions and the other devoting itself primarily to the creation of eternal values. In the former there may be opulent living in terms of ephemeral goods and starvation in terms of eternal goods—eating, drinking, and wallowing in entertainment, in sordid, ugly, mean, and unhealthy surroundings; while in the latter, there may be frugal living in terms of ephemeral goods and opulence in terms of eternal goods—modest, simple, and healthy consumption in a noble setting. In terms of conventional economic accounting they are both equally rich, equally developed—which merely goes to show that the purely quantitative approach misses the point.

The study of these two models can surely teach us a great deal. It is clear, however, that the question: 'Which of the two is better?' reaches far beyond the economic calculus, since quality cannot be calculated.

No one, I suppose, would wish to deny that the life-style of modern industrial society is one that places primary emphasis on ephemeral satisfactions and is characterised by a gross neglect of eternal goods. Under certain immanent compulsions, moreover, modern industrial society is engaged in a process of what might be called 'ever-increasing ephemeralisation'; that is to say, goods and services which by their very nature belong to the eternal side are being produced as if their purpose were ephemeral. The economic calculus is applied everywhere, even at the cost of skimping and cheese-paring on goods which should last for ever. At the same time, purely ephemeral goods are produced to standards of refinement, elaboration, and luxury, as if they were meant to serve eternal purposes and to last for all time.

Nor, I suppose, would anyone wish to deny that many preindustrial societies have been able to create superlative cultures by placing their emphasis in the exactly opposite way. The greatest part of the modern world's cultural heritage stems from these societies.

The affluent societies of today make such exorbitant demands on the world's resources, create ecological dangers of such intensity, and produce such a high level of neurosis among their populations that they cannot possibly serve as a model to be initiated by those two-thirds or three-quarters of mankind who are conventionally considered underdeveloped or developing. The *failure of modern affluence*—which seems obvious enough, although it is by no means freely admitted by people of a purely materialistic outlook—cannot be attributed to affluence as such, but is directly due to mistaken priorities (the cause of which cannot be discussed here): a gross over-emphasis on the ephemeral and a brutal under-valuation of the eternal. Not surprisingly, no amount of indulgence on the ephemeral side can compensate for starvation on the eternal side.

In the light of these considerations, it is not difficult to understand the meaning and feasibility of a culture of poverty. It would be based on the insight that the real needs of human beings are limited and must be met, but that their wants tend to be unlimited, cannot be met, and must be resisted with the utmost determination. Only by a reduction of wants to needs can resources for genuine progress be freed. The required resources cannot be found from foreign aid; they cannot be mobilised via the technology of the affluent society which is immensely capital-intensive and labour-saving and is dependent on an elaborate infrastructure which is itself enormously expensive. Uncritical technology transfer from the rich societies to the poor cannot but transfer into poor societies a life-style which, placing primary emphasis on ephemeral satisfactions, may suit the taste of small, rich minorities, but condemns the great, poor majority to increasing misery.

The resources for genuine progress can be found only by a life-style which emphasises frugal living in terms of ephemeral goods. Only such a life-style can create, maintain and develop an ever-increasing supply of eternal goods.

Frugal living in terms of ephemeral goods means a dogged adherence to simplicity, a conscious avoidance of any unnecessary elaborations, and a magnanimous rejection of luxury—puritanism, if you like—on the ephemeral side. This makes it possible to enjoy a high standard of living on the eternal side, as a compensation and reward. Luxury and refinement have their proper place and function but only with eternal, not with ephemeral, goods. This is the essence of a culture of poverty.

One further point has to be added: the ultimate resource of any society is its labour power, which is infinitely creative. When the primary emphasis is on ephemeral goods, there is an automatic preference for mass-production, and there can be no doubt that mass production is more congenial to machines than it is to people.

The result is the progressive elimination of the human factor from the productive process. For a poor society, this means that its ultimate resource cannot be properly used; its creativity remains largely untapped. This is why Gandhi, with unerring instinct, insisted that "it is not mass production but only production by the masses that can do the trick." A society that places its primary emphasis on eternal goods will automatically prefer production by the masses to mass production, because such goods, intended to last, must fit the precise conditions of their place: they cannot be standardised. This brings the whole human being back into the productive process, and it then emerges that even ephemeral goods (without which human existence is obviously impossible) are far more efficient and economical when a proper 'fit' has been ensured by the human factor.

All the above does not claim to be more than an assembly of a few preliminary indications. I entertain the hope that, in view of increasing threats to the very survival of culture—and even life itself—there will be an upsurge of serious study of the possibilities of a culture of poverty. We might find that we have nothing to lose and a world to gain.

[1]In unpoetical English: 'Even as a child I fell terror-struck when I heard it said that to live an agreeable life you have got to be rich.'
[2]Cf: E.F. Schumacher 'Roots of Economic Growth', Gandhian Institute of Studies, Varanasi, India, 1962, pp 37/38.

Vol 6 No 1, Mar-Apr 1975

INDUSTRY

Industry & Morals

EVERYBODY WISHES TO BELIEVE that there must be a technical or scientific solution to every problem: a technical solution as against a moral one, something which the brain can work out without the participation of the heart. For social ills, bring in the sociologist; for economic ills, the economist; for physical ills, the doctor; and so forth. The ideal is to reduce every problem to a mathematical statement or formula, so that, once this has been done, nobody any more has to use even his brain, let alone his heart or his feelings, to find the correct solution: to find it, can be left to a calculating machine, a computer. Since some problems, particularly those arising from inanimate nature—in physics, chemistry, astronomy, engineering—can be very effectively dealt with in this manner: why not all problems? Why not equally those arising from animate and human nature? This is the current thinking, and there is some truth in it; but not enough.

It seems to me, therefore, that the obligations of Christian men and women in modern society extend beyond personal conduct, that is, the practice of such fundamental virtues as patience and generosity, and include an intellectual effort of a pretty severe kind (and here I use the word "intellectual" in its old sense to comprise not only the functions of the calculating reason but also those powers of intuition and insight which precede and transcend reason). The task is to discriminate and thereby to put everything into its proper place. All ills arise from something being in the wrong place, being out of proper focus. If you get it back to where it belongs, the ill disappears. Every Christian knows the truth (enshrined in all the languages with which I am acquainted) that "whole", "wholesome", and "holy" are, to say the least, closely interrelated.

Let us see what all this means in practical terms. Christianity teaches us to put things in the right place, in the right order of priority if you like. Right thinking comes before, and is the precondition of, right action. One of the great, incredible formulae of Christianity, known to all of us is this: "Seek ye first the Kingdom of God, and his righteousness, and all these things"—all these other things which you also need, the economic things—"shall be added unto you". Another great formula, equally well known and today equally incredible, is the assertion that "Man shall not live by bread alone, but by every word that proceedeth out of the mouth of God".

However we may wish to interpret sayings such as these, we cannot fail to see that they set up an order of priority which is the opposite of what modern industrial man is normally inclined to think and do. The formula by which we, collectively, live today could perhaps be put like this: "Seek ye first to achieve a higher rate of economic growth, and its material benefits, and heaven on earth will follow by itself."

Which of the two formulae is true? They cannot both be true. Many opposites, I know, can exist side by side, but two opposite orders of priority cannot both be true. In the end, the test must be a pragmatic one, in accordance with the saying that "Ye shall know them by their fruits".

Well, then, can we apply such a test? How are we to set about such a task? Are we to put all the fruits of the modern way of life on a huge pair of scales, the good ones on one side and the bad ones on the other, and then see which side outweighs the other? How are we to weigh the ugliness of our cities against the convenience afforded by washing machines? Even a computer would not enable us to do this.

Is there another way? The problem, after all, is far from unique. Everybody, for instance, is concerned that there should be "a fair reward for a fair day's work". Yet we cannot define fairness. Our power of judgement is insufficient to obtain the positive, but it just suffices to recognise the negative. Even though we cannot define justice or fairness, we can recognise injustice and unfairness. An attempt to establish the former can never succeed; the only approach to success is made by fighting the latter.

Similarly, we cannot weigh the good fruits of our civilisation against the bad fruits; but we can none the less identify the bad fruits and fight against their causes.

All this presupposes, of course, that we can adequately distinguish between good and bad—at least at the extremes. And this, I believe, is where the specific contribution of the Christian must come in, and where his contribution today seems to be woefully inadequate.

To distinguish, to discriminate, not to fall for the general clap-trap, the plausible and silly slogans, in short, to see things as they really are and to name them accordingly; which means to see things against a full and comprehensive picture of Man: this is the task of Christians.

What is Man?—surely, the most relevant, the most practical question anyone can ask. Could it be, for instance, that our economic ills are due to a fragmentary, distorted, unwholesome and therefore unholy picture of man? The full picture includes not only what he is but also what he could be and ought to be. It is not a picture that can be drawn by positivistic science alone. One of the fragmentary pictures of man is that of the current Religion of Economics. Man is there seen, primarily and essentially, as a consumption machine; the criterion of his worth is his so-called standard of life, meaning the amount of stuff he is managing to consume in a year. And since, collectively, his consumption depends upon his production, he is simultaneously seen as a producing machine; the criterion of his worth being his production, his productivity. The criteria of the worth of a whole society are the Gross National Product and its annual rate of growth. A famous passage in *The Affluent Society* by J. K. Galbraith, discussing the "second-best" year in American history, describes this outlook as follows:

> ". . . no person. . . showed the slightest disposition to challenge the standard by which it is decided that one year is better than another. Nor was it felt that any explanation was required. No one would be so eccentric as to suppose that second best meant second best in the progress of the arts and sciences. No one would assume that it referred to health, education, or the battle against juvenile delinquency. There was no suggestion that a better or poorer year was one in which the chances for survival amidst the radioactive furniture of the world had increased or diminished. . . Second best could mean only one thing—that the production of goods was the second highest in history."

And another American sums it up from another angle:

"Any device or regulation which interferes, or can be conceived as interfering, with (the) supply of more and better things is resisted with unreasoning horror, as the religious resist blasphemy, or the warlike pacifism."

Homo œconomicus, man seen as a production & consumption machine, is a distorted, fragmentary, unholy and unwholesome picture of man. It is also one which has far-reaching practical consequences. In this country, few people have been more explicit in their warnings on this point than Professor R. H. Tawney. He said that a philosophy which holds "that the attainment of material riches is the supreme object of human endeavour and the final criterion of human success. . . is the negation of any system of thought or morals which can. . . be described as Christian", and he warned us that "to convert efficiency from an instrument into a primary object is to destroy efficiency itself".

Let us consider this last statement. Is it true? What evidence is there that societies pursuing efficiency as a primary object are destroying efficiency itself? Is America doing so, or Germany? Surely, Tawney's statement is unduly pessimistic?

To test the statement against the facts, it is necessary to see the whole performance of society, not merely its industrial performance. One way of raising productivity is to draw people from agriculture into industry and from the country into the cities. Here is a recent report from *Time* magazine:

"Barely two centuries have sufficed to bring U.S. cities to desperate crisis. With seven out of ten Americans now living in cities, the U.S. is the world's largest urban society. The growth of the cities has been so swift that it has spawned some of the nation's deepest and most pressing problems. Throughout the U.S., the big cities are scarred by slums, hobbled by inadequate mass transportation, starved for sufficient finance, torn by racial strife, half-choked by polluted air. . . the Great Society can hardly stand on a foundation of urban decay."

Where is the efficiency of the arrangement as a whole? Los Angeles provides an outstanding illustration. "Los Angeles county now has 3,900,000 autos for a population of 7,000,000, and the number is growing faster than the human population. There is little public transport; less than 8% of Angelenos travel to and from work by public transport." (Time, 2nd Sept. '66) Taken by itself, the American car industry is, of course, highly efficient; but how could this efficiency ever offset the monstrous inefficiency of needing nearly 4 million cars for 7 million people? As a professor from California once put it to me: "This does not indicate a high standard of living, but the terrible cost of transportation."

Another American author, Mr. Lewis Herber, says this:

"The modern city has reached its limits. Megapolitan life is breaking down psychologically, economically, and biologically. Millions of people have acknowledged this breakdown by 'voting with their feet', they have picked up their belongings and left (for suburbia). . . The reconciliation of man with the natural world is no longer merely desirable; it has become a necessity. . ."

What Mr. Herber is saying is that the heedless pursuit of efficiency has produced a pattern of living which is highly inefficient in human terms: it robs people of their real freedom, and they vote against it with their feet.

They also vote against it in other ways. How could anyone overlook the fact that crime, in Britain no less than in America, is growing at a much faster rate than Gross National Product? Crime is becoming a big economic phenomenon, with an annual turnover approaching that of the largest industries. President Johnson, a year or so ago, proposed a "National Strategy against Crime" and stated in a message to Congress:

"We know (the cost of crime) in dollars, some $27,000 million (nearly £10,000 million) annually. We know the still more widespread cost it exacts from millions in fear; fear that can turn us into a nation of captives. . . fear that can make us afraid to walk the city streets by night or public parks by day. These are costs a truly free people cannot tolerate."

In Britain, the number of indictable offences known to the police has trebled, from 400,000 to 1,200,000 in less than 12 years. Year after year, the highest rates of increase are in the age groups from 14 to 21. Who are the criminals? Not, in general, people lost in poverty and unemployment; but people in some kind of revolt; or people for whom the strains of life have become intolerable. There are other reactions to strain, other forms of escapism: drug addiction, for instance, or mental breakdown. According to estimates produced by the chairman of the National Association for Mental Health in Britain,

> "one in every nine girls aged six now will enter a mental hospital at some time in her life, and one among every fourteen six-year-old boys."

I shall not weary you with a complete listing of all forms of breakdown and escapism—all of them rapidly increasing. The generally accessible facts suggest that Tawney may not have been far wrong when he asserted that to pursue efficiency as a primary object will produce such inefficiencies as to destroy efficiency itself, or when he warned us that unless economic life satisfied criteria which were not purely economic, it would be "paralysed by recurrent revolts".

Economic growth is no antidote to these ominous manifestations. If pursued as a primary aim, if idolized as the most essential task of society, it bears bitter fruit and tends to defeat itself. Set it up as the supreme national objective, and you will inevitably promote greed, impatience, ruthlessness and envy, destroying those fundamental virtues without which no society can function satisfactorily.

Economic growth, in itself, is neither a good thing nor a bad thing. It all depends on what is growing and what is being displaced or destroyed. Never has it been more necessary than in our time to apply distinctions and use discrimination. Unlimited science and unlimited engineering are putting ever more powerful forces at the disposal of somebody. Who are these somebodys? What are they doing with these forces? What motivates them? Are they good men or evil men, or perhaps indifferent men primarily concerned with pursuing their own careers? If they are given the simple and crude objective of "faster economic growth", can they distinguish between healthy and unhealthy growth? Do they care for their fellow men? Do they care for God-given Nature or do they think of it as a quarry for exploitation? Do they know the truth of what St. Thomas Aquinas said 700 years ago and would no doubt repeat today, that the smallest mosquito is more wonderful and mysterious than anything made by man?

An attempt to answer these questions leads one to facts which are far from reassuring. The spirit of violence and impatience has invaded wide ranges of scientific work, producing a flood of innovations of an increasingly dangerous character. The pressures of rivalry, competition and ambition are such that only the minimum of time is allowed for an examination of consequences. The God-given environment is subjected to unlimited degradation until the legislator steps in, normally at a very late stage, to stop the grossest abuses.

This ruthless application of partial knowledge, stimulated by impatient demands for faster growth, quicker returns, and greater speed, now constitutes such a direct threat to human health and happiness that even quite ordinary people, without knowledge of the scientific details, are looking into the future with a deep, often sub-conscious dread. The idolaters of growth, of course, treat this dread with ridicule, contempt, and hatred; but that does not help; on the contrary, it merely drives it deeper.

Why are teenagers and juveniles showing the highest growth rates in crime and other symptoms of revolt, escapism, or breakdown? Is it because they have the longest future to dread? Can we take it lightly that so many of them now refer to their participation in adult life as "joining the rat race"? There could hardly be a greater sign of human failure than this.

When people set out to build the Tower of Babel to reach the very sky, the Lord allowed them to fall into confusion. We live, indeed, in confusing times. The Religion of Economics has conquered almost the entire world, yet in its hour of triumph increasing numbers of people—and the young in particular—revolt against it by refusing to accept its disciplines. We preach the virtues of hard work and restraint, while painting utopian pictures of unlimited consumption without either work or restraint. We complain when an appeal for greater effort meets with the ungracious reply: "I couldn't care less", while promoting dreams about automation to do away with manual work and about the computer to relieve men from the burden of using their brains. When a minority will be "able to feed, maintain and supply the majority, it makes no sense to keep in the production stream those who have no desire to be in it", said a recent Reith lecturer. Many there are who have no desire to be in it, because the work they have to do is of no interest to them, provides them with neither challenge nor satisfaction, and has no other merit in their eyes than that it leads to a pay packet at the end of the week. If our intellectual leaders treat work as nothing but a necessary evil, soon to be abolished as far as the majority is concerned, the urge to minimise it right away is hardly a surprising reaction.

A recent book on 'Religious Faith and Twentieth Century Man' demonstrates our confusions in an almost comical fashion. It opens with the normal flourishes: "Twentieth Century man no longer has the same sense of his own inadequacy and helplessness as his forebears had. . . he feels himself, as never before, the master of his fate, and is intent, by his own efforts. . . on creating a better world". It then proceeds to a lament about increasing uncertainty of how to create order out of the modern chaos. "We now live," says the author, "in an age of huge impersonal groupings. . . more and more reducing people to things. . . Everywhere man is faced with hugeness, in which he is a mere impersonal unit and which he cannot control." The former statement is the myth maintained by intellectuals out of touch with ordinary people; the latter describes accurately what the majority of Twentieth Century men experience in their daily lives. And as Tawney pointed out forty years ago: "Since even quite common men have souls, no increase in material wealth will compensate them for arrangements which insult their self-respect and impair their freedom."

It is the task of scientists to discover the laws of nature; of inventors to invent; of industrialists to set up and organise useful production; and of government to govern. But none of these activities, no matter how specialised, can be wholesome unless carried on by people who take full responsibility for their actions, being imbued with a fully developed sense of the sacredness of all existence—a knowledge that they have not made the world and have not made themselves. No one can be a specialist without also being a man, and man has responsibilities which are wider than those arising from his specialised pursuits It is absurd to claim absolute rights for anything contingent, be it science, power, or economic growth, and the inevitable result of absurdity is confusion. No way out of confusion exists, except by the patient and generous rebuilding of a true order of priorities, a true scale of values.

To do this, I believe, is the task of Christians, wherever life may have placed them. They are not *against* economic growth any more than they would be against science or government. But they are against the Zeitgeist which tends to make idols of these contingent things. They are critical, not of this subject or that, but of the spirit that informs the specialists working in their chosen fields. If that spirit is impatient, violent, ungenerous, or narrow, the fruits will be poisoned, no matter what the initial appearances might suggest.

Do you wish me to give specific examples? I shall give three. A spirit of violence of the most ruthless kind has invaded man's agricultural activities. It has been courageously and brilliantly exposed in two publications by women, Miss Rachel Carson and Mrs. Ruth Harrison in their books *Silent Spring* and *Animal Machines*. The arguments that followed the publication of these books have been highly instructive. They seldom rose above the level of technical discussion or sentimentality. "Don't worry, where there are benefits, there is always a price to be paid. After all, what do these lay-people know about such highly technical matters anyhow?— Who can prove that animals suffer when kept in darkened boxes all their lives and fed a deficiency diet to make their flesh, whiter?—Insecticides and pesticides are essential to modern agriculture and, a few accidents or abuses apart, can never do any harm—If the balance of nature is upset, if wildlife suffers, if insects or germs develop new resistant strains: scientific progress will know how to cope with any eventually." It is truly a case of the bland leading the blind. Yet one does not have to be an expert to see a spirit of violence at work which puts man in a wrongful relationship with God's creation. It is hardly an exaggeration to say that modern factory farming has about it an air of baseness bordering on criminality. And this at a time when increasing numbers of people are making almost desperate efforts to find relief from city strain by an escape into the countryside. They are feeling, as Lewis Herber put it, "a growing need to restore the normal, balanced, and manageable rhythms of human life"—that is, an environment in which the violence of mechanical gigantism is replaced by the gentle patience of natural, biological processes.

The spirit of impatience and violence ruled the earlier phases of the industrial revolution in an appalling fashion and is still endemic in modern industry. This is inevitably so, and it would be futile to complain about it. Every Christian in industry knows it and suffers from it. But he can nevertheless work for its mitigation. The problem of how to humanise work, how to restore the human group structure to industrial organisation, is certainly a difficult one. Some tendencies in modern technology, such as decentralised power, are helpful, others are inimical. One can try and favour the former and resist the latter. Computers, which all too easily could promote gigantism, can also be used to decentralise operations into human-scale group activities. An intensive study of these possibilities, I believe, should be a primary concern of Christian men. But it is quite clear that the urgent and necessary work along these lines will not be done if the exclusive concern of industry is held to be efficiency.

On a still wider canvas, we notice a heedless spirit of violence with regard to the natural resources needed for industrial production. Fuel resources furnish the outstanding example. We do not make them but take them out of Nature's larder. What we have taken, is gone; and if we take ruthlessly, going only for what is cheapest to take, we spoil even more than we take. We do not have the patience to be conservationists. As George Kennan once put it, we behave as if we had no past and no future.

The obligation on the Christian in this economic age is to keep his eyes open and recognise the evils which result from an inverted order of priorities. He is not against science, power, or wealth, as I have said already. But he knows that these are means, and not ends, and are of value only if they serve man—that strange, undefinable being about whom we know so much and yet so little. One thing we do know about him on the highest authority, namely, that it shall profit him nothing to gain the whole world if, in the process, he loses his soul.

Vol 2 No 5, Jan-Feb 1969

Technology & Political Change

FEW PEOPLE DENY that technological change has political consequences; yet equally few people seem to realise that the present
'system', in the widest sense is the product of technology and cannot be significantly changed unless technology is changed.

The question may be asked: What is it that has produced modern technology? Various answers can be given. We may go back to
the Renaissance, or even further, to the arising of Nominalism, and
point to certain changes in Western man's attitude to religion, science, Nature, and society, which then apparently released the intellectual energies for modern technological development. Marx and
Engels gave a more direct explanation: the rising power of the
bourgeoisie, that is, 'the class of modern capitalist, owners of the
means of social production, and employers of wage labour'.

> "The bourgeoisie, wherever it has got the upper hand, has put
> an end to all feudal patriarchal, idyllic relations. It has pitilessly
> torn asunder the motley feudal ties that bound man to his
> 'natural superiors', and has left no other bond between man and
> man than naked self-interest, than callous 'cash payment' . . . It
> compels all nations, on pain of extinction, to adopt the bourgeois
> mode of production.
>
> The bourgeoisie has subjected the country to the rule of
> the towns. It has created enormous cities . . . has agglomerated
> population, centralised means of production, and has concen-
> trated property in a few hands."

If the bourgeoisie did all this, what enabled it to do so? The
answer cannot be in doubt: the creation of modern technologies.
Once a process of technological development has been set in
motion it proceeds largely by its own momentum irrespective of
the intentions of its originators. It demands an appropriate system,
for inappropriate systems spell inefficiency and failure. Whoever
created modern technology, for whatever purpose, this technology

or, to use the Marxian term, these modes of production, now demand a system that *suits them*, that is appropriate to them.

As our modern society is unquestionably in crisis, there must be something that does not fit:

(a) If overall performance is poor despite brilliant technology, maybe the 'system' does not fit.

(b) Or maybe the technology itself does not fit present-day realities, including human nature.

Which of the two is it? This is a very crucial question. The assumption most generally met is that the technology is all right—or can be put right at a moment's notice—but that the 'system' is so faulty, it cannot cope: "Modern bourgeois society with its relations of production, of exchange and of property, a society that has conjured up such gigantic means of production and of exchange, is like the sorcerer who is no longer able to control the powers of the nether world whom he has called up by his spells . ... The conditions of bourgeois society are too narrow to comprise the wealth created by them. And how does the bourgeoisie get over these crises? On the one hand by the enforced destruction of a mass of productive forces; on the other, by the conquest of new markets and by the more thorough exploitation of the old ones. That is to say, by paving the way for more extensive and more destructive crises, and by diminishing the means by which crises are prevented." (Marx and Engels: Manifesto of the Communist Party, 1848). The culprit is the Capitalist System, the Profit System, the Market System, or, alternatively, nationalisation, bureaucracy, democracy, planning or the incompetence of the bosses. In short: we have a splendid train but a bad track or a rotten driver or a lot of stupid, unruly passengers. Maybe all this is quite true, except that we do not have such a splendid train at all. Maybe what is most wrong is that which has been and continues to be the strongest formative force—the technology itself. If our technology has been created mainly by the capitalist system, is it not probable that it bears the marks of its origin, a technology for the few at the expense of the masses, a technology of exploitation, a technology that is class-orientated, undemocratic, inhuman, and also unecological and non-conservationist?

I never cease to be astonished at the docility with which people—even those who call themselves Socialists or Marxists—accept technology, uncritically, as if technology were a part of Natural Law. As an example of this 'docility' we may take the Prime Minister of Iran who is reported to have said in a recent interview (*To the Point International*, January 12, 1976):

> "There are many aspects of the West that we particularly wish to avoid in the industrialisation of Iran. *We seek the West's technology only, not its ideology.* What we wish to avoid is an ideological transplant."

The implicit assumption is that you can have a technological transplant without getting at the same time an ideological transplant; that technology is ideologically neutral; that you can acquire the hardware without the software that lies behind it, has made the hardware possible, and keeps it moving. Is this not a bit like saying: I want to import eggs for hatching, but I don't want chicks from them but mice or kangaroos'!

I do not wish to overstate the case; there is nothing absolutely clear-cut in this world and, no doubt, many different tunes can be played on the same piano, but whatever is played it will be piano music. I agree with the general meaning of Marx's rhetorical question: "Does it require deep intuition to comprehend that man's ideas, views, and conceptions—in a word, man's consciousness— changes (he does not say: is totally determined) with every change in the conditions of his material existence, in his social relations and in his social life?"

It is a great error to overlook or to underestimate the effects of the 'modes of production' upon people's lives, not just their 'standard of living':

- how they produce; what they produce;
- where they work; where they live; whom they meet
- how they relax or 'recreate' themselves; what they eat, breathe, and see;
- and therefore what they think, their freedom or their dependence.

Adam Smith was under no illusion about the effects of the 'mode of production' on the worker: "The understandings of the greater part of men are necessarily formed by their ordinary employments. The man whose whole life is spent in performing a few simple operations. . . has no occasion to exert his understanding. . . He naturally loses, therefore, the habit of such exertion and generally becomes as stupid and ignorant as it is possible for a human creature to become . . . but in every improved and civilised society this is the state into which the labouring poor, that is, the great body of the people, must necessarily fall, unless government takes some pains to prevent it."

Marx, who quotes Adam Smith, adds the comment that "some crippling of body and mind is inseparable even from division of labour in society as a whole. Since, however, manufacture carries this . . . much further and also, by its peculiar division, attacks the individual at the very roots of his life, it is the first to afford the materials for, and give start to industrial pathology." And he quotes his contemporary, D. Urquhart, who says: "The subdivision of labour is the assassination of a people."

People still say: it is not the technology: it is the 'system'. Maybe a particular 'system' gave birth to this technology: but now it stares us in the face that the system we have is the product, the inevitable product, of the technology. As I compare the societies which appear to have different 'systems', the evidence seems to be overwhelming that where they employ the same technology they act very much the same and become more alike every day. Mindless work in office or factory is equally mindless under any system.

I suggest therefore that those who want to promote a *better* society, achieve a *better* system, must not confine their activities to attempts to change the 'superstructure'—laws, rules, agreements, taxes, welfare, education, health services, etc. The expenditure incurred in trying to buy a better society can be like pouring money into a bottomless pit. If there is no change in the base—which is technology—there is unlikely to be any real change in the superstructure.

People say to me: before you can make headway with your 'Intermediate Technology' you must first change the system, do away with capitalism and the profit motive, dissolve the multinationals, abolish all bureaucracies, and reform education. All I can reply is: I know of no better way of changing the 'system' than by putting into the world a *new type* of technology—technologies by which small people can make themselves productive and relatively independent.

During the eighteenth and nineteenth centuries technology just grew like Topsy. Increasingly, however, it became the outgrowth of Science. Today, its primary derivation is from Science; in fact, it appears that Science is today mainly valued for its technological fruits.

Starting, then, with Science, the question may be raised: what determines the course of Science'? There is always more that *could* be studied than *can* be studied: so there is need for choice, and how is it made?

By the interests of scientists? Yes, unquestionably.
By the interests of big business and government ? Surely yes.
By the interests of 'the people'? On the whole, no!

The people have fairly simple requirements to meet for which hardly any additional science is needed. (It could be that an entirely different kind of science would really benefit the people; but that is another matter.)

Moving on from Science to Technology, there is again far more that *could* be done than *can* be done. The choice is endless. Who decides or what decides? Scientific findings can be used for, 'incarnated in', countless different 'shapes' of technology, but new technologies are developed only when people of power and wealth back the development. In other words, the new technologies will be in the image of the system that brings them forth, *and they will reinforce the system*. If the system is ruled by giant enterprises— whether privately or publicly owned—the new technologies will tend to be 'gigantic' in one way or another, designed for 'massive breakthroughs', at massive cost, demanding extreme specialisation, promising a massive impact—no matter how violent—'we shall know how to cope with the consequences'. The slogan is: 'a breakthrough a day keeps the crisis at bay'. We hear of 'white hot technological revolution', the Nuclear Age, the Age of Automation, the Space Age, fantastic feats of engineering, supersonic triumphs, all that; but many of the most basic needs of great masses of people, such as housing, cannot be taken care of.

The most telling example, of course, is the most advanced society of the modern world, the United States. Average income per head is over twice that of Britain or Western Europe, and yet there is more degrading poverty the States than you can ever see in Europe;

5.6% of the world population using something like 35% of the world's output of raw materials—and not a happy place: great wealth in some places but utter misery, degradation hopelessness, strife, criminality, escapism, sickness of body and mind almost everywhere; it is hard to get away from it. How is it possible—in a country that has more resources, more science and technology than anybody ever had in human history? People are questioning everything, every part of the superstructure—big business, big government, big academia; and very gradually, hesitantly, at long last they are beginning to question the basis of it all—technology.

Technology Assessment Groups have sprung up in various places; they 'assess' technological developments mainly in the light of three questions:

- What does it do in terms of resource usage?
- What does it do to the Environment?
- What is its socio-political relevance ?

Concorde did not fare well under their scrutiny. They concluded that it was wasteful of scarce resources, environmentally burdensome and even dangerous and socio-politically irrelevant. It may none the less be described as a marvellous achievement of Anglo-French engineering.

Let us follow through a few of the structural effects of modern technology. Its effect on the nature of work has already been referred to. It is, l believe, the greatest destructive force in modern society. What could be more destructive than the destruction of people's understanding? Matters have not improved since Adam Smith's time; on the contrary, the relentless elimination of creative work for the great majority of the population has proceeded apace.

What has been the effect of modern technology upon *the pattern of human settlement*? This is a very interesting subject which has received hardly any attention. Professor Kingsley Davis, world-famous authority on urbanisation, says: "The world as a whole is not fully urbanised, but it soon will be." He, like the UN and the World Bank, produces indices of urbanisation showing the percentage of the population of different countries living in urban areas (above a certain size). The interesting point is that these indices entirely miss the interesting point. Not the degree but the *pattern* of urbanisation is the crux of the matter. Human life, to be fully human, needs the city; but it also needs food and other raw materials gained from the country. Everybody needs ready access to both countryside and city. It follows that the aim must be a *pattern* of urbanisation so that every rural area has a nearby city, near enough so that people can visit it and be back the same day. No other pattern makes human sense.

Actual developments during the last 100 years or so, however, have been in the exactly opposite direction: the rural areas have been increasingly deprived of access to worthwhile cities. There has been a monstrous and highly pathological polarisation of the pattern of settlements. The French planners fight against France becoming 'Paris surrounded by a desert'; in the United States they have coined the term 'megalopolis' to describe the vast conurbations which have arisen while the life has been seeping out of small and medium-sized country towns. There is 'Boswash', extending from Boston to Washington DC; there is 'Chicpitts', a conurbation stretching from Chicago to Pittsburgh: and there is 'Sansan', from San Francisco to San Diego. Even in the United Kingdom, often referred to as a tightly packed little island, the pattern of settlement is extraordinarily lop-sided, with more than half the area grossly under-populated and large parts of the other half madly congested.

Do you remember this socialist demand, formulated more than 100 years ago?—

> Combination of agriculture with manufacturing industries; gradual abolition of the distinction between town and country by a more equable distribution of the population over the country. (*Communist Manifesto*, 1848).

And what has happened during those more than 100 years? Of course the exact opposite. And what is expected to happen during the next twenty-five years to the end of the century? Again the exact opposite, with a vengeance. Not urbanisation but, to use a word as dreadful as the phenomenon it denotes, *megalopolitanisation*, a movement that produces as we know only too well utterly insoluble political, social, moral, psychological and economic problems.

A paper issued by the World Bank speaks of: "the despondency surrounding the task of ameliorating urban conditions in the developing countries (which) arises primarily from the speed of urban growth and shortage of resources, human as well as financial. . . Urban administration is woefully lacking in capacity to deal with the problems. . . Yet within less than twenty years the present populations and areas of urban centres will account for less than a third of the total." The paper asks whether there is a possibility "of accelerating the development of small and medium-size towns or creating new urban growth centres". But it loses little time in dismissing this possibility: "Most small urban centres. . . lack the basic infrastructure of transport and services. . . Management and professional staff are unwilling to move from the major cities." This tells the whole story: "Management and staff are unwilling to move from the major city!" The proposition, evidently, is to transplant into a small place the technology which has been developed in such a way *that it fits only a very large place*. The people in the small place cannot cope with it; management and staff have to be imported from the 'major cities'; no one wants to come because the proposition does not make economic sense. The technology is inappropriate and that means the whole project is uneconomic.

With a name like mine I find it easy to understand that to be a good shoemaker it is not enough to know a lot about making shoes; you also have to know about feet. The shoe made for the big fellow does not fit the foot of the little fellow. The small foot needs a different shoe, *not an inferior one* but one of the right size. Modern technology, generally speaking, makes good shoes only for big fellows. It is geared to mass production; it is highly sophisticated and enormously capital-costly. Of course it does not fit anywhere but in or near the biggest cities or megalopolitan areas.

The simple answer to this problem does not seem to have occurred to many people. It is: let us mobilise at least a small part of our intellectual and other resources to create a technology that *does* fit the smaller places.

Incredible amounts of money are being spent in trying to cope with the relentless growth of megalopolitan areas and in trying to infuse new life into 'development areas'. But if you say: "spend a little bit of money on the creation of technologies that *fit the given conditions of development areas*," people accuse you of wanting to take them back into the Middle Ages.

One thing, however, can be asserted with confidence: unless

suitable appropriate technologies for efficient production *outside* the main conurbations are created, the destructive tendencies of 'megalopolitanisation' will continue to operate with all that this implies socially, politically, morally, environmentally, and resource-wise.

Having traced the effect of modern technology upon the nature of work and the pattern of human settlement, let us now consider a third example, a highly political one, its effect on human freedom. It is undoubtedly a tricky subject. What is freedom? Instead of going into long philosophical disquisitions, let us ask the more or less rebellious young what they are looking for.

Their negations are such as these:

I don't want to join the rat race.
Not be enslaved by machines, bureaucracies, boredom, ugliness.
I don't want to become a moron, robot, commuter.
I don't want to become a fragment of a person.

Their affirmations?

I want to do my own thing.
I want to live (relatively) simply.
I want to deal with people, not masks.
People matter. Nature matters. Beauty matters. Wholeness matters. I want to be able to care.

All this I call a longing for freedom.

Why has so much freedom been lost? Some people say: "Nothing has been lost, but people are asking for more than before." Whichever way it is, there is a gap between supply and demand of this most precious thing—freedom. Has technology anything to do with this? The size and complexity of organisations certainly has a great deal to do with it.

Why is the trend of the last 100 years towards bigger and bigger units? Nobody except a few monomaniac tycoons likes them. Why do we have to have them? The invariable answer is: because of technological progress. And why don't our engineers produce technological progress in another direction:

• towards smallness

- towards simplicity
- towards capital-cheapness
- towards technological non-violence?

If we ask the engineers, the answer is: "Because nobody has ever asked us for it." And if you ask: "Can it be done?", the answer is: "Of course it can be done if there is a demand for it."

Not very long ago I visited a famous institution developing textile machinery. The impression is overwhelming. The latest and best machines, it seemed to me, can do everything I could possibly imagine; in fact, more than I could imagine before I saw them.

"You can now do everything," I said to the professor who was taking me around, "why don't you stop, call it a day?"

My friendly guide did indeed stop in his tracks: "My goodness!" be said "what do you mean? You can't stop progress. I have all these clever people around me who can still think of improvements. You don't expect me to suppress good ideas? What's wrong with progress?"

"Only that the price per machine, which is already around the £100,000 mark, will rise to £150,000."

"But what's wrong with that?" he demanded. "The machine will be 50% dearer but at least 60% better."

"Maybe," I replied, "but also that much more *exclusive* to the rich and powerful. Have you ever reflected on the *political* effect of what you are doing?"

Of course, he had never given it a thought. But he was much disturbed; he saw the point at once. "I can't stop," he pleaded.

"Of course you can't stop. But you can do something all the same: you can strive to create a counterweight a counterforce, namely, efficient small-scale technology for the little people. What are you in fact doing for the little people?"

"Nothing."

I talked to him about what I call the 'Law of the Disappearing Middle'. In technological development, when it is drifting along, outside conscious control, all ambition and creative talent goes to the frontier, the only place considered prestigious and exciting.

Development proceeds from Stage 1 to Stage 2, and when it moves on to Stage 3, Stage 2 drops out; when it moves on to Stage 4, Stage 3 drops out and so on.

It is not difficult to observe the process. The 'better' is the enemy of the good and makes the good disappear *even* if most people cannot afford the better for reasons of Money, Market, Management or whatever it might be. Those who cannot afford to keep pace drop out and are left with nothing but Stage 1 technology. If, as a farmer, you cannot afford a tractor and a combine harvester, where can you get efficient animal-drawn equipment for these jobs—the kind of equipment I myself used thirty-five years ago? Hardly anywhere. *So you cannot stay in farming.* The hoe and the sickle remain readily available; the latest and the best—for those who can afford it—is also readily available. But the middle, the intermediate technology, disappears. Where it does not disappear altogether it suffers from total neglect—no improvements, no benefits from any new knowledge, antiquated, unattractive, etc.

The result of all this is a loss of freedom. The power of the rich and powerful becomes ever more all-embracing and systematic. The free and independent 'middle class' capable of challenging the monopolistic power of the rich disappears in step with the 'disappearing middle' of technology. (There remains a middle class of managerial and professional servants of the rich organisations; they cannot challenge anything.) Production and incomes become concentrated in fewer and fewer hands or organisations or bureaucracies—a tendency which redistributive taxation plus ever-increasing welfare payments frantically try to counteract—and the rest of mankind have to hawk themselves around to find a 'slot' provided by the rich, into which they might fit. The First Commandment is: Thou shalt adapt thyself. To what? To the available 'slots'. And if there are not enough of them available, you are left unemployed. Never previously having done your own thing, it is unlikely that you will have the ability to do it now, and in any case the technology that could help you to do your own thing *efficiently* cannot be found.

What is the answer'? The 'Law of the Disappearing Middle' in *technology has to be counteracted by conscious work*, namely by the development of 'intermediate technologies' striving for

- smallness
- simplicity
- capital-cheapness

• non-violence

The fourth criterion, being somewhat different in kind from the first three, may require some further elucidation. To cite an extreme example, consider the political implications of the most violent technology ever developed, nuclear energy—'peaceful' nuclear energy. Consider the security measures required when plutonium and other radioactive material becomes ubiquitous as it will if present plans for nuclear expansion are implemented. These terrible substances must never leak into the environment; must never get out of control in any way; and must never fall into the wrong hands—of blackmailers, terrorists, political desperados or suicidal maniacs. There will be a continuous flow of traffic crisscrossing the country, taking these materials through their various stages of processing and use—and nothing must ever go seriously wrong. The connection between technology and freedom is obvious and it is not difficult to see that the price of freedom, or at least an important part of it, *is the avoidance of violent technologies.*

Vol 7 No 4, Sept-Oct 1976

Chapter 11

Western Europe's Energy Crisis

IT IS IMPOSSIBLE TO EXAGGERATE the dependence of the modern world on fossil fuels. As these fuels are non-renewable and constitute a once-for-all endowment of the earth, their availability in terms of quantity, and therefore also of time, is limited, and it must give rise to increasingly serious concern that the modern economy seems to be inexorably geared to a continuous, exponential growth in its requirement for them. In 1971—the latest year for which global statistics have been assembled—total world energy consumption amounted to 7,260 million tons of coal equivalent, nearly 300 million tons more than in 1970, and of this total oil and natural gas accounted for 64 percent, solid fuel for 34 percent, and primary electricity (i.e. hydroelectricity and nuclear energy) for two percent. Thus fossil fuels, which strictly speaking are non-reproducible 'capital', supplied 98 percent of all requirements, while reproducible 'income fuels' supplied only two percent. It can be argued that this understates the contribution of the latter; by the application of different conversion factors, 'income fuels' could be shown to contribute six percent of the total. But this does not alter the basic situation of virtually total dependence on 'capital'.

The geographical distribution of fossil fuel reserves as well as that of fuel demand, exacerbates the situation. From the point of view of demand *versus* resources, the world may be divided into four groups of countries—Group 1 with high consumption rates and large indigenous resources; Group 2 with high consumption rates and small resources; Group 3 with low consumption rates and large resources; Group 4 with low consumption rates and small resources. The outstanding representatives of Group 2 are Western Europe and Japan, while the United States of America is rapidly moving into a similar position. The outstanding representatives of Group 3 are the Middle East and North Africa. The relationship between these two groups is of crucial importance—at least in the short run of the next ten to thirty years. The countries of Group 3 are increasingly becoming aware of their immense bargaining power—which they have solidified by setting up OPEC, the Organisation of the Petroleum Exporting Countries, and they are also becoming aware of the enormous difficulties encountered in developing an alternative livelihood for their populations, to be available when their oil reserves run out. Having discovered that the demand for their oil is virtually inelastic even at steeply rising prices, they can obtain more money by releasing less oil, and many of them already find themselves with a greater foreign exchange income than they can spend on imports. What are they to do with their cash surpluses? They are gradually coming to the conclusion that the best long-term investment for them may be to leave the oil in the ground and release it only at the rate determined by their foreign exchange needs. These developments, so far gradual but none the less implacable, are placing the countries of Group 2 in a position of immediate danger.

No one can predict how soon severe supply curtailments will set in, but this is no reason for pretending that all is well for 'the foreseeable future'. Nor can anyone say with certainty what the 'ultimate reserves' of fossil fuels might be. Calculations about ultimate reserves, which normally include even the hydrocarbons contained in shales and tar sands, only serve to divert attention from the immediate dangers. All new developments—as we have seen with nuclear energy—have a 'lead time' extending over decades rather than years before they can be brought to a quantitatively relevant scale. In this connection *scale is* decisive, and it should never be forgotten that the *annual increment* in the world's fossil fuel requirements is a magnitude counted in many hundreds of millions of tons of coal equivalent. Even if there is no question of a total and permanent stop in the flow of oil supplies from the OPEC countries, a temporary interruption due to political factors, or a significant permanent reduction could play havoc with the economies of Group 2 countries and cause a degree of paralysis and disorder from which it might be extremely difficult to recover.

In view of these basic facts, here only very broadly sketched, there is now a growing realisation in Western Europe, Japan, and other countries of Group 2 of the need to search for new 'energy policies'. In principle, such policies would fall into two classes—those designed to enlarge alternative sources of supply and those designed to reduce demand. Let us first look at the demand side. Needless to say, steeply rising oil prices will, to some extent, curtail demand, but, as already mentioned, fuel demand is highly inelastic, because *fuel is primarily a means of production for which there is no substitute and no possibility of recycling, so that going without fuel means going without production.* The most expensive fuel, one might say, is the fuel one cannot get when one needs it. There are, of course, many possibilities of improving the technical efficiency of fuel and energy utilisation, which during the era of cheap fossil fuel supplies have been somewhat neglected. But it would be fanciful to attribute to these possibilities a decisive quantitative significance: their realisation requires very large capital investments—as for instance in the utilisation of waste heat from existing power stations—and what is more, a great deal of time. There is no realistic possibility for improvements in fuel efficiency to do more than slightly reduce the rate of *increase in* total fuel and energy demand. To try and do so is, of course, helpful; but it cannot be expected to make more than a marginal contribution. *The question needs to be asked: What accounts for the extraordinarily high level of fuel and energy consumption in the so-called advanced countries, while traditional societies seem to be able to get along with very small fuel inputs indeed?* The answer normally given simply refers to the higher level of income of the former. But this answer is too superficial. Take, for instance, the production and consumption of foodstuffs. In 'advanced' societies the production process requires fuel and energy inputs which are a high multiple of those required by traditional societies, although food consumption levels are *not* very much higher in the former than in (some of) the latter. A study of these situations provides some valuable pointers. Similar pointers can be obtained from historical analysis. During the last twenty-five years, for instance, the fuel requirements of agriculture in the advanced countries, including the fuel requirements of agricultural inputs as well as those of food processing have increased by a far higher factor than the increase in agricultural output.

Why is it that agriculture—per unit of output—has become so enormously more 'fuel dependent'? The answer can be found only in the emergence of:

- new patterns of production;
- new patterns of consumption; and
- new patterns in the geographical distribution of populations.

American studies have shown the enormous dependence of American agriculture on fossil fuels. "Harvested crops capture solar energy and store it as food or some other useful product. Yet the energy captured is small compared to the energy we burn to capture it. *Agriculture, has become a major consumer of our stores of energy, using more petroleum than any other single industry.* If the world is facing a future with rising energy prices the highly mechanised technology currently used in US agriculture may be inappropriate."[1] Professor Barry Commoner has given some telling figures:

> "In 1949, an average of about 11,000 tons of fertilizer nitrogen were used per. . . unit of crop production, while in 1968 about 57,000 tons of nitrogen were used for the same crop yield. This means that the efficiency with which nitrogen contributes to the growth of the crop declined fivefold."[2]

During the same period, the US population increased by 34 percent; total US agricultural production rose by 45 percent; *the annual use of fertilizer nitrogen increased by 648 percent*, and the harvested area *declined* by 16 percent.[3] During a similar period, between 1946 and 1971, *the proportion of the American working population engaged in agriculture fell from 14 percent to 4.4 percent.* It is in these changes in the *pattern of production*, not in any inefficiency of fuel utilisation in mechanical equipment or chemical factories, that an explanation of agriculture's enormous dependence on fossil fuels must be sought.

The patterns of consumption have been changing in a similar way. In the advanced countries, very little food reaches the consumer in its natural state. Virtually all foodstuffs are elaborately processed, packaged, and transported over long distances. With the growth of specialised mass production, consumption has become widely separated from production—and all this requires prodigious amounts of cheap mechanical and process energy.

While agriculture serves as a particularly telling example, because human food consumption is biologically limited and does not grow significantly with growing affluence, the same tendencies can be observed in industry and, in fact, in all other parts of the modern economy. They are being further promoted by changing *patterns in the geographical distribution of populations*, of which urbanisation is the most important. Everywhere, most glaringly in the developing countries, fossil fuel consumption rates per capita are highest in the big cities, and this applies to all sectors—domestic, industrial, transport, public utilities, etc. Although specific statistical information is hard to come by, it can hardly be doubted that *within* each country there is a highly positive correlation between *per capita* fuel consumption and 'density'.

It follows from these considerations, and from the factual evidence, that a significant reduction in the dependence of a modern society on fuel supplies can be achieved only by means of the evolution of a new life-style—with new patterns of production, new patterns of consumption, and new patterns as regards the geographical distribution of the population. Inasmuch as the present-day life-style has been shaped largely by modern technology, it would seem unlikely that a different life-style could emerge without the conscious and deliberate creation of new 'styles of technology'.

Before considering this matter we have, however, to have a look at the supply side: What are the possibilities of developing alternative sources of fuel supply to fill the gap if oil should become scarce? When this question is raised, people are inclined to point to the allegedly unlimited possibilities of nuclear energy. *As long as no method exists for the safe disposal of radioactivity, any large-scale development of fission energy would be nothing short of suicidal.* Such a large-scale development, it must also be emphasised, would be possible only on the basis of breeder-reactors. However, "the expected switch to fast breeder reactors will aggravate the situation even further, for they produce large quantities of radioactive substances with very long half lives."[4] It has also been observed that "one of the most disturbing features of nuclear generators in current use is that exhausted reactor cores cannot be dismantled, but must be sealed and buried. . . People are seriously worried about risks of exposure to radiation, either through accidents of unimaginable dimensions or through the cumulative effect of small doses, directly experienced or indirectly transmitted."[5]

And "breeder reactors are inherently more difficult to control because the process takes place much faster"[6] than in any of the reactors now in use. In view of these appalling dangers, there is now a good deal of talk about the limitless possibilities of fusion energy. "Generation by nuclear fusion produces no radioactive wastes. . . The difficulty is that the process only works continuously at enormously high temperatures (up to 200 million °C)".[7] What the massive production of sun temperatures on earth would do to the living environment is completely unknown; but, in any case, the practical feasibility of such a process applied on a quantitatively relevant scale has in no way been established, so that no realistic policies can be based on the expectation of its successful implementation within the foreseeable future.

The discussion therefore turns to the possibility of the large-scale utilisation of solar energy and its derivatives, and also of tidal power and geothermic heat. These sources of 'income energy' are, of course, very large, inexhaustible (with some reservations regarding geothermic heat), and extremely widely spread over the globe. The difficulty is that, being widespread they are inherently diffuse and cannot easily be concentrated or centralised into large and continuous supplies, such as the modern world is used to with fossil fuels. *The question of solar energy immediately raises the question of 'life-style' as alluded to above. Highly diffuse energy would fit only a highly decentralised mode of living.* We are therefore brought back to the proposition that the modern world's dependence on fossil fuels could be significantly reduced only by means of the development of new 'styles of technology'.

It is at this point that we might with advantage turn our attention to the position of the Third World, most of which belongs to Group 4—countries with low energy consumption rates and small indigenous fuel resources. The development policies of the last twenty years have been virtually exclusively based on the assumption that 'development' can be most speedily achieved by transferring the high technology of the rich countries to the Third World. Where this transfer has been effected, the result has been a concentration of development upon big cities; a massive migration of rural populations into these cities which consequently have become infested with enormous slums; mass unemployment; stagnation of life in the rural areas; and sharply increasing energy requirements. The view is now gaining ground that what the Third World needs more urgently than anything else is an 'appropriate technology', although there is as yet little understanding as to what constitutes 'appropriateness'. What emerges ever more clearly from the work of the Intermediate Technology Development Group, is that one of the primary criteria of 'appropriateness' is 'small-scale'. Most people of the Third World still live in villages and small towns, and they cannot possibly be absorbed into cities. Local markets are generally small, both on account of decentralised living and on account of poverty, which means that large-scale mass-production industry cannot economically be fitted into the rural areas. Small markets demand small-scale production units, and these can be viable only on the basis of an efficient small-scale technology. Practical work on the development of such technologies has already established their feasibility, provided that the best resources of modern science and technical knowledge are deployed to this end.

In view of the gravity of the energy problem with which the advanced societies of Group 2 are faced, any work undertaken in this direction cannot but turn out to be of the greatest possible relevance also to their own problems of survival.

People have to have food before they can do anything else; the most urgent need, therefore—whether from the point of view of fighting hunger in the Third World today, or of developing new life-styles in the advanced countries to meet possible oil scarcities tomorrow—is a reconsideration of agricultural methods and policies. *At least agriculture should be relatively independent of fossil fuels, which means independence of large-scale mechanisation and intensive chemicalisation.* At least agriculture should be so organised that it can, in case of crisis, absorb large amounts of labour, thereby giving large numbers of people the chance of making a living. There is no branch of production more suitable for the intelligent utilisation of solar energy and other 'income fuels' and also for the systematic practice of 'recycling'. Nor do we have to look for entirely 'new models' if we want to develop a truly self-supporting agriculture. Many successful farmers around the world, in rich countries as well as in poor, are today obtaining excellent yields without mammoth mechanisation and without using any products of the chemical and pharmaceutical industries. Their methods are properly attuned to the cycle of nature which, as we all know, requires no other fuel input but that of solar energy.

It may seem surprising that a consideration of energy policy has taken us 'back to the soil' and thus 'back to nature'. But this is quite inevitable if we wish to move from the surface of the problem to its root. The mortal weakness of the modern world lies in its alienation from the unalterable facts of nature, one manifestation of this alienation being its heedless reliance on fossil fuels. What has been said above is not meant to suggest that putting agriculture on a basis of permanence would, by itself, provide a solution of the energy problem. It does mean to suggest however, that no solution can be found in terms of energy technology and economics—or energy power politics—alone and that the challenge presented by the energy problem is one of developing a new life-style—a development which logically and inevitably must begin with a change of our relation to the soil, of which we are a product and which alone sustains our lives.

References
1. CBNS Notes, (Center for the Biology of Natural Systems, Washington University, St Louis, Missouri) Volume 6,1, 5 (1973). 2. B. Commoner, *The Closing Circle* (Alfred A Knopf, New York 1971), pp 149-150. 3. ibid. 4. *Pollution: Nuisance or Nemesis?* (London, HMSO 1972), p 36. 5. *Sinews for Survival* (London, HMSO 1972), pp 37-38. 6. ibid, p 36. 7. ibid, p 36.

Vol 5 No 3, July-Aug 1974

DEVELOPMENT

✍ Chapter 12 ✍

Healthy Development

BY WAY OF INTRODUCTION, a short report from East Africa:

The Dutch manager of the textile plant received me with the greatest courtesy and not at all with the suspicion and irritated resentment I had half expected. "Another official visitor," he might well have thought, "to steal my time and ask more or less irrelevant questions." And, of course, I was going to ask plenty of questions.

"This plant, as you will see, is highly automated", he said.

"Before you go on," I interrupted, "could you just explain one thing to me. As I was coming in I noticed some hundred or so young African men at the factory gates, and armed guards keeping them out. Is this a riot or something?"

The Dutchman laughed: "Oh no! They are always there. They hope that I might sack someone and that they could step into his job."

"So you have quite a bit of unemployment in this town?"

"Yes, terrible."

"Thank you; excuse the interruption. Please carry on."

"This plant, as you will see," said the Dutchman, "is one of the most modern in East Africa, highly automated. We employ about 500 people, but this is much too much. We hope to get the number down quite considerably as our automated equipment becomes fully operative."

"So there is not much hope for the chaps outside?"

"No, I am afraid, there isn't."

"Tell me, what would be the total capital value of a plant like this?"

"About £11 million."

"For 500 jobs," I calculated aloud, "this means about £3,000 per workplace. That's a lot of money for a poor country, the sort of 'capital intensity' we have in Western Europe or the United States."

"Yes indeed," said my Dutch friend, "my plant is as modern as you would find anywhere in the world."

He must have noticed my astonishment.

"You see," he continued, "we have to be competitive. The quality demanded today is very high. I cannot afford to send out faulty material. It is terribly difficult to train these people here to work faultlessly, they have no tradition of industrial discipline. Machines make no mistakes, human beings do. To get a high quality product we must eliminate the human factor."

"I quite understand," I said, "but tell me this: why has this factory been placed in this small town? Surely, you would be better off, marketwise and in every other respect, in the capital city?"

"Indeed we would. We did not want to come here. This was a planning decision of the Government."

"What was their reasoning?"

"Very simple", he said. "There is a lot of unemployment in this region. So we had to come here."

"I see. And your aim is to eliminate the human factor?"

"Yes", said the Dutchman. "I can see there is a conflict here. But I have to make this investment pay. What can I do?"

The problem is two-fold: how to obtain faster development and how to obtain healthy development. On a superficial view, the two parts of the problem are in conflict; on a deeper view, they are complementary, except in the very short term.

Evidence of unhealthy development exists all over the world, including some of the richest countries. It leads to a degradation of people and a ruination of the environment. Development is healthy only if it leads to an upgrading of people on the widest possible scale and an upgrading of their environment also on the widest possible scale.

What is the main cause of 'development' going wrong? It is the neglect of the geographical (locational) factor. While all development work is difficult it is much easier in the big city—normally the capital city—than in the secondary towns; in the bigger towns, than in the little towns; and it is most difficult in the rural areas.

The free play of economic forces invariably favours the urban as against the rural areas, the big towns as against the small. It tends to produce the triple disease of mass migration into cities, mass unemployment, and the danger of famine.

Mushrooming cities, surrounded by ever-growing misery-belts, infested by a largely unemployed proletariat without nourishment for body or soul can be found all over the world. For a rich minority, they offer the high life of extravagant luxury, albeit under the shadow of personal insecurity owing to the prevalence of crime and the symptoms of political instability. For the destitute majority they offer nothing but degradation.

The rural areas, meanwhile, tend to sink into ever deeper decay. Every gifted person tries to migrate into the city, to escape from rural misery, and this irresistible 'brain drain' makes the problems of the rural hinterland ever more intractable. At the end of this kind of 'development' lies social chaos, the degradation of man and of his environment.

Most developing countries are overwhelmingly agricultural and must obviously give primary emphasis and attention to the development and upgrading of their agriculture. As agriculture cannot be practised in towns, it is the rural areas that must receive the main emphasis and attention.

What kind of emphasis and attention? It is of little use to go to semi-literate peasants engaged in primitive subsistence farming and expect them to adopt and successfully to practise modern farming methods. Poverty is a vicious circle; it feeds upon itself. The vicious circle of rural poverty can be broken only by introducing non-agricultural activities into the rural areas. These activities may be summed up in two words: industry and culture.

Agriculture alone, at the level of poverty, consisting as it does of scraping the ground and living with cattle, cannot develop the mind. Agricultural populations need the stimulus of non-agricultural activities, or they will stay at the subsistence level and increasingly tend to desert the land in the hope of finding a 'better life' in the cities.

Without culture, agricultural practices cannot be upgraded and industry cannot be established. Culture is primary; it leads by itself to industrial development which, in turn, helps to stimulate culture.

If this is accepted, the strategy of development becomes clear: first and foremost, bring culture into the villages; at the same time, bring industry. (By 'villages' I mean communities with at least a few hundred, but preferably a few thousand inhabitants. Widely scattered hamlets cannot be helped at this stage.)

To put this in another way: Everything needs a certain 'structure'. Culture needs a consciously evolved structure just as industry needs a consciously evolved structure. In both cases, the 'structure' must be qualitative and at the same time geographical, if it is to be a healthy one.

An ideal cultural structure would look like this: a number of cultural 'units' make up the country, each of them containing at least one million and at the most, say, three million inhabitants. Each cultural 'unit' is a pyramid, as follows: primary schools at the village level; a number of villages headed by a market town with a secondary school, a number of market towns headed by a regional centre with an institution of higher learning.

An ideal industrial structure would be essentially similar: small-scale industries in the villages; medium-scale industries in the market towns; large-scale industries in the regional centres; and perhaps a few exceptional and unique industrial activities in the capital city (although this is by no means essential, since the capital city provides in any case certain non-industrial services to the country, which are themselves 'exceptional and unique').

I am not suggesting that such ideal structures are attainable in every case; but they do provide guidelines. It is also obvious that 'industry' is more closely tied to location factors than culture, so that the industrial structure will have to tolerate more 'deviations from the ideal' than the cultural structure.

It must be emphasized that there are no master-key solutions to the problem of healthy development. Gigantic schemes, whether in agriculture, industry, communications, or even in education, may seem attractive in theory but are invariably disastrous in practice. The key to success is not mass production but production by the masses. Any purely economic assessment of a proposed new activity is bound to be misleading, unless the political, sociological, and geographical requirements and prevailing conditions are clearly stated and accepted as terms of reference. The economic calculus by itself always tends to favour the large project as against the small; the urban project as against the rural, the capital-intensive project as against the labour-intensive, because the task of managing machines is always easier than that of managing people. But this simply means that the economic calculus is applicable only after the basic policy decisions have been taken. These basic policy decisions should favour the small project as against the large; the rural project as against the urban; the labour-using project as against the capital-using—until labour becomes the effective bottleneck.

Three lines of effort have to be pursued simultaneously in a strategy of healthy development:

(a) bring culture into the rural areas;
(b) bring industrial activities into the rural areas; and
(c) upgrade agricultural methods and practices.

(a) *Culture*

The elements of culture are visual matter, music, reading matter, industrial skills (which will be dealt with separately), and body culture, i.e. hygiene and sport. In all these respects the rural areas are poverty-stricken. To mend this state of affairs demands a great deal of leadership and only a relatively small amount of money.

If Government offices look dilapidated, dirty, and drab, then Government will not be convincing when it calls upon the people to make their houses and villages look smart, clean, and colourful. Self-reliance presupposes a certain pride, and pride grows on the basis of cleanliness and smartness. Whitewashed houses are an asset only if they are kept whitewashed. Wherever possible, bring paint into the villages.

Local art is a major instrument of development. It stimulates the mind, and that is the starting point of everything.

Self-made music, which is better than radio, is both a stimulus and an attraction.

Most important of all: reading matter. After literacy—what? For every 20 shillings spent on education in literacy, it is worth while, and indeed necessary, to spend at least one shilling on the preparation, production, and distribution of reading matter. This must not be confined to utilitarian, instructional material, but must include material of wider scope—political, historical, artistic—a systematic 'Feed-the-Minds Programme'.

Hygiene and sport are equally essential instruments of development.

In all these matters, not only the men but also the women need to get involved. If anything, the women are more important than the men, as the next generation is in their care.

How can this be accomplished? It cannot be done by a few education or committee development officers, but only by a systematic involvement of the entire educated population of the developing country.

These few remarks about culture had to be made because it is too often overlooked that culture and not money, is the primary motive power of development.

The sense of isolation in the rural areas and small towns is intensified by the lack of newspapers and other reading material. The newspapers produced in the capital city normally reach the hinterland only irregularly and often with considerable delay. They are also too expensive.

With a bit of local initiative and central support, small local news-sheets could be produced very cheaply.

A successful scheme practised in one developing country was as follows: A number of fairly well educated people from small towns and large villages in the hinterland—mainly school teachers —were given a short training course in the capital. After training, they were supplied with a 'do-it-yourself kit', consisting of a transistor radio (if they did not possess one already), a typewriter, a simple hand-duplicator, and a fair stock of suitable paper. It was arranged that the central radio station would broadcast, three time a week, a News Bulletin at dictation speed. The people trained for this purpose went back to their towns and villages, tuned in at the arranged times, and produced a duplicated news-sheet at minimal expense three times a week. The scheme turned out to be financially self-supporting. In some cases, the local news sheet producer found it possible to add local news and even editorial matter.

Reading matter is one of the main instruments of culture and, in fact, an indispensable one. Without it, all education is abortive. It can be very cheaply produced. But the contents must be appropriate to the actual conditions of people living in poverty. (People no longer living in poverty have the means to look after themselves). Apart from news, the poor need 'simple messages', that is, small pamphlets with printed matter and visual supports which describe down-to-earth possibilities of self-help and self-improvement—how to build a small feeder road; how to improve one's house; how to feed oneself and the children; how to practise elementary hygiene;

also how to paint, make music, and so forth.

To produce such 'simple messages' is not easy. Indigenous academics and other intellectuals should organize themselves in small spare-time study groups to prepare them. No one else can do it. But they have to be conscious of the three great gulfs that separate them from the poor in the hinterland and that have to be bridged by compassionate care—the gulf between the rich and the poor; the gulf between the educated and the uneducated; and the gulf between the townsman and the countryman.

(b) *Industry*

Opportunities for industrial development exist wherever people live together in hundreds or thousands. They also exist wherever valuable raw materials can be found or produced.

Assuming there is an established population of several hundred thousand people, inhabiting a district or region in a not-too-scattered fashion industrial development depends on the following factors:

(1) Local initiative and will to work along new lines;
(2) Technical know-how, including the knowledge of local natural resources;
(3) Commercial know-how;
(4) Money.

In the rural areas and small towns, all these factors are scarce, and industrial development depends not only on their fullest mobilization but also on their systematic, planned supplementation from outside.

As I have said before, poverty is a vicious circle, and all beginnings are difficult. To look for opportunities for industrial activities means therefore, initially at least to look for activities in which a beginning has already been made, and to build on them.

The first task is to study what people are already doing—and they must be doing something, otherwise they could not exist—and to help them to do it better, which often means to help them to advance from raw material production into the successive stages of processing.

The second task is to study what people need and to investigate the possibility of helping them to cover more of their needs out of their own productive efforts.

It is only when these two tasks have been successfully accomplished that one can safely advance to a third task, that is, to produce new articles destined for markets outside.

Local initiatives for self-help and self-improvement are the most precious asset of all, because without them no organic growth can take place. A population without such initiatives is almost impossible to help. It follows that all such initiatives, wherever they arise, deserve the most careful and sympathetic nurturing and the maximum of outside support.

Appropriate industries in the hinterland will rarely need large amounts of capital, because they will be modest in size and will rarely require more than a few hundred pounds of capital investment per person employed. The lower the average amount of the capital to be found for each industrial workplace, the more workplaces can be created by the investment of a given amount of money. Only by creating a large number of low-cost work places can the problem of mounting unemployment be solved.

It cannot be emphasized too strongly that this is a matter of conscious political choice and not one to be decided by the calculations of economists or businessmen. A country's development policy may be geared primarily to the production of goods or it may be geared primarily to the development of people. The former aims at mass production, the latter, at production by the masses. The former is the inevitable result, if private enterprise is given a free hand, because it is the natural, i.e. rational, desire of the private enterprise employer 'to eliminate the human factor', for the simple reason that automated machinery works faster and more reliably than any human being. Feasibility studies undertaken by politically 'neutral' economists will always support this tendency, particularly in a developing country where labour, being unused to industrial work, has yet to be trained. It is then argued that mass production, once successfully established, will benefit the masses by the provision of cheap consumer goods. But since mass production at the level of high capital intensity 'eliminates the human factor', the masses find themselves unemployed and unable to buy even the cheapest goods. It is claimed that mass production, if it does find a market, is the most effective instrument for the rapid accumulation of surplus wealth, and that this surplus will then 'percolate' to the unemployed masses. Yet it is a fact of universal experience that no such 'percolation' takes place; a 'dual economy' emerges in which the rich get richer while the poor stagnate or get poorer. Under such auspices, 'self-reliance', 'involvement of the people', and 'development' must remain ineffectual aspirations.

If the political decision is in favour of production by the masses—rather than mass production which 'eliminates the human factor'—it follows automatically that the difficult task of developing industrial activities in the hinterland must receive top priority, simply because the mass of the people happen to live in the hinterland and it would be a disaster if they (or even a sizeable proportion of them) were drawn into the capital city. It also follows that industrial developments in the capital city should be strictly confined to two categories, 'national plants' (in certain cases) and small production units serving the local market.

By 'national plants' I mean unique enterprises at a high level of sophistication and capital intensity which for one reason or another cannot be established in the hinterland; an obvious example would be a plant concerned with the servicing of international airliners, but there are no doubt other legitimate cases. Industries in the capital city should be capital-intensive and labour-saving, because it is not desirable to draw people into the capital city by creating large numbers of industrial workplaces there. Industries in the hinterland should be labour-intensive and capital-saving, because it is desirable to hold the population in the hinterland and give them the chance of acquiring industrial skills.

(c) *Agriculture*

It is now widely accepted that in the generality of cases farming in a poor country cannot straightaway move from the hoe to the tractor, or from the panga to the combine harvester. An 'intermediate' stage must first be reached and consolidated, utilizing equipment that is very much more efficient than hoe or panga and very much cheaper and easier to maintain and utilize than tractor or combine.

The question is: how is the farmer or the farming community to choose the equipment appropriate to their specific needs, how are they to obtain supplies, including spare parts, and how are they to pay for them? The farmer's basic implements are plough, harrow, planter, cultivator, and cart. Some of these can be made by local carpenters, to appropriate specifications, e.g. the harrow and the cart. The others have to be obtained from merchants, who may have to import them. Normally the merchants are unable to offer the farmer a wide enough choice of implements for instance, of ploughs. Nor is the farmer always in a position to judge which type of plough is suitable for his soil and other circumstances. If he has only two oxen, a plough needing four to six oxen to pull it is a disaster for him. The wrong depth of ploughing may be equally fatal.

In every developing country arrangements along the following lines are required: First, agricultural extension officers need to have at their disposal a whole range of appropriate equipment, such as ploughs, so that, going from farm to farm, they can determine—and demonstrate—which particular type of plough is appropriate to the given conditions. Second, there must be an organization capable of manufacturing or importing the appropriate equipment, including spare parts, and organizing its distribution. There is often no alternative to a governmental organization undertaking this very urgent task. Third there is generally a need to increase and intensify the education of farmers in the training of draught animals and the use and maintenance of animal-drawn equipment.

If healthy development requires a strategy as outlined above—a strategy in which the governments of the developing country have to take all the decisive initiatives—what kind of help can and should be given by the rich countries? It is obvious that it is easy to produce or promote unhealthy development—just provide some funds and let things happen as they will. Most of the so-called development will then continue to go into the capital cities; the rich will get richer; the poor, poorer. There will be mass production, instead of production by the masses. The ablest, most progressive, most dynamic and up-to-date business men will 'eliminate the human factor' and the economists and statisticians will celebrate splendid 'rates of growth'. All this is relatively easy—and it is the road to a sickness which even the richest societies may find it hard to survive.

But healthy development, with production by the masses instead of mass production, with the cultivation, instead of the elimination, of the human factor, with only modest urbanization and an organic agro-industrial structure in the hinterland, based on self-reliance and the involvement of the people—that is a different matter. Are we fit to help? Or are we so much caught up in our own system of 'eliminating the human factor' that ours will inevitably and inescapably be the withering touch of which there is so much evidence already?

We can help them with our knowledge, but not with the ways in which we ourselves have utilized and exploited our knowledge. We can help them to solve their problems; if we merely offer them the solutions of our problems, we ruin them.

As Professor Myrdal has emphasized in his stupendous work *Asian Drama: an Inquiry into the Poverty of Nations*, the technological advance in the West is very detrimental to the development prospects of the Third World, and there is little hope unless "its unfortunate impact could be counteracted by deliberately increasing research activity and directing it towards problems the solution of which would be in the interest of the under-developed countries".

But who will support those who are struggling to work along such lines? Increasing numbers of people realize that such work is necessary but they do nothing to help it along.

The poor cannot be helped by our giving them methods and equipment which presuppose a highly developed industrialism. They need an 'intermediate technology'; they need the stepping stones of self-help.

The Intermediate Technology Development Group in London is organizing this kind of 'help to help them help themselves'. It is a group of scientists, administrators and businessmen, who believe that the scientific knowledge and worldly competence of the affluent West can be organized to help the poor countries without destroying their identity and self-respect.

Vol 2 No 8/9, July-Oct 1969

Industrialisation through intermediate technology

AN IMMEDIATE CAUSE of much misery and frustration in many 'developing' countries is undoubtedly unemployment, particularly in rural areas. This generally gives rise to mass migration into metropolitan areas. It is possible to speak of a 'process of mutual poisoning'. The establishment of modern industry in a few metropolitan areas tends to kill off competing types of traditional production throughout the countryside, thus causing widespread unemployment or under-employment. The countryside thereupon takes its revenge by mass migration into the metropolitan areas, causing them to grow to a totally unmanageable size.

Current forecasts on the growth of metropolitan areas in the 'developing' countries suggests that few people expect this destructive process of mutual poisoning to be stopped or mitigated. Very few people indeed appear to expect that even the most ambitious 'rates of economic growth' could suffice to cope with the problem of unemployment during the foreseeable future, exacerbated as this problem is being by the so-called population explosion. Fifteen and even twenty-five year 'perspective plans' have been published in various 'developing' countries which appear to hold out no hope of economic integration for the majority of people in these countries. In fact, the longer the forecast, the more desperate the situation appears to become, with towns growing to a size of 20, 40 and even 60 million inhabitants, a prospect of 'immiseration' for multitudes of people that beggars the imagination.

It may be mentioned in passing that the trend towards 'megalopolis', towards vast conurbations, coupled with the denudation of the countryside, has recently been recognised as a serious problem even in the most highly developed countries such as the United States, Britain, France and Italy. These countries may be able to shoulder the colossal economic burdens arising therefrom, although the question remains whether developments of this kind really represent a rational and desirable employment of economic wealth. Whether or not the social fabric of the wealthy countries can carry these burdens, it seems abundantly certain that the 'developing' countries cannot recover economic health along this road. No doubt, national incomes can grow and will continue to grow; but statistics of this kind do not necessarily signify a nation's 'standard of life': they may merely give evidence of its rising 'cost of subsistence'. It is undeniable that a man's 'cost of-subsistence' rises significantly the moment he moves from a rural area into a big town where he becomes dependent on a multitude of costly public services which the rural environment provides free of charge.

'Economic growth', a purely quantitative concept without any qualitative determination, cannot be accepted as a rational- objective of policy. The problem is how to obtain healthy growth. Experience shows that there are types of economic growth which spell increasing misery for ever more people and destroy all social cohesion. Many 'developing' countries already suffer from internal economic divisions which are euphemistically called the 'dual economy', where there are in fact two different patterns of living as widely separated from one another as two different worlds. It is not a question of some people being rich and others being poor, both being united by a common way of life: it is a question of two ways of life existing side by side in such a manner that even the humblest member of the one disposes of a daily income which is-a high multiple of the income accruing to even the hardest working member of the other. The social tensions arising from the 'dual economy' are today evident in many, if not all, of the 'developing' countries.

Again in passing, it may be mentioned that tendencies in this direction are recognisable even in the 'richest country in the world', the United States, which have moved President Johnson to declare a 'War on Poverty' to rescue from misery some 38 million Americans! It appears therefore that immensely strong forces of a disruptive kind are being let loose by certain modern developments of the economy. America may deploy massive wealth to cope with them; but how are the 'developing' countries to master them without massive wealth?

The experts rarely refer to the twin evils of mass unemployment and mass migration into towns in the 'developing' countries. When they do so, they merely deplore them and treat them as 'transitional'. Yet there is no evidence at all that time alone will be the great healer. In case after case unemployment is greater at the end of a Five-Year Plan than it had been at the beginning. India is a case in point and so is Turkey. Developing countries "cannot include the goal of full employment among their immediate planning targets", says a recent study published in the International Labour Review. They cannot, so it is argued, because they are short of capital. As they cannot conquer unemployment, so they cannot conquer mass migration, and as their towns grow to an ever more monstrous size they tend to absorb what little capital there is just to maintain more people in misery.

There is need, it seems, for some fresh thinking. It might help to remember certain fundamental truths, such as the undeniable fact that 'capital' consists primarily of tools and machines, the purpose of which is to save work, or to lighten it, or to enable people to accomplish more through it. A lack of capital, therefore, should not mean less, but on the contrary, more work for people—more work, albeit less productive work. Even work of low productivity is more productive than no work at all. Why should we accept that 'lack of capital' makes unemployment inevitable? Lack of capital today means lack of modern machinery. Was there mass unemployment before the advent of modern machinery? Was there a mass flight from the land in the now-developed countries before the industrial revolution? To pose these questions does not mean to solve the problem as it faces us today, but it may help to make a constructive solution visible.

It would seem that the primary task of the 'developing' countries—and also of the givers of foreign aid—is to go straight into battle with the twin evils of mass unemployment and mass migration into cities. This means:

First, that workplaces have to be created in the areas where the people are living now, and not primarily in metropolitan areas into which they tend to migrate;

Second, that these workplaces must be, on average, cheap enough so that they can be created in large number without this calling for an unattainable level of savings and imports;

Third, that the production methods employed must be relatively simple, so that the demands for high skills are minimized, not only in the production process itself but also in matters of organisation, raw material supply, financing, marketing, and so forth; and

Fourth, that production should be largely from local materials for local use.

These four requirements can be met only

(a) if there is a 'regional approach' to development, and
(b) if there is a conscious effort to develop what might be called an 'intermediate technology'.

A given political unit is not necessarily of the right size as a unit for economic development. If vast and expensive population movements are to be avoided, each 'district' with a substantial population needs its own development. To take a familiar example, Sicily does not develop merely because Italian industry, concentrated mainly in the North of the country, is achieving high rates of economic growth. On the contrary, the developments in the North of Italy tend to increase the problems of Sicily through their very success by competing Sicilian production out of existence and draining all talented and enterprising men out of Sicily. If no conscious efforts are made to counteract these tendencies in some way, success in the North spells ruination in the South with the result that mass unemployment in Sicily forces the population into mass migration. Similar examples could be quoted from all over the world. Special cases apart, any 'district' within a country, if it is being bypassed by 'development', will inevitably fall into mass unemployment, which will sooner or later drive the people out.

In this matter it is not possible to give hard and fast definitions. Much depends on geography and local circumstances. A few thousand people, no doubt, would be too few to constitute a 'district' for economic development. But a community of a few hundred thousand people, even if fairly widely scattered, may well deserve to be treated as a development district. The whole of Switzerland has less than six million inhabitants; yet it is divided into more than twenty 'cantons', and each 'canton' is a kind of development district, with the result that the tendency towards the formation of vast industrial concentrations is minimised.

Each 'district', ideally speaking, would have some sort of inner cohesion and identity and possess at least one town to serve as the district centre. While every village would have a primary school, there would be a few small market towns with secondary schools, and the district centre would be big enough to carry an institution of higher learning. There is need for a 'cultural structure', just as there is need for an 'economic structure' within any country, be it even as small as Switzerland. This need for internal 'structures' is of course particularly urgent in large countries, such as India. Unless every district of India is made the object of development efforts, so to say: for its own sake and in its own right, all development will concentrate in a few places with devastating results for the country as a whole.

It is obvious that this 'regional' or 'district' approach has no chance of success unless it is based on the employment of suitable technology. We have already alluded to the disruptive forces, stemming from modern technology, which are making themselves felt even in the most highly industrialised countries today. The trend to 'megalopolis' noticeable all over the world, is simply the effect of modern technology, in transport as well as in industrial production, which lives under the law of 'nothing succeeds like success'. Unfortunately, the inevitable concomitant of this law is its opposite: 'Nothing fails like failure', and this gives rise to the twin evils of unemployment and mass migration in the 'developing' countries. The only chance of counteracting these baneful laws would seem to be the conscious development of an 'intermediate technology'.

Here again, it is not possible to arrive at any simple and clear-cut definition. 'Intermediate technology' must be appropriate to the country in question. It is surely an astonishing error to assume that the technology developed in the West is necessarily appropriate to the 'developing' countries. Granted that their technological backwardness is an important reason for their poverty; granted, too, that their traditional methods of production, in their present condition of decay, lack essential viability: it by no means follows that the technology of the richest countries is necessarily suitable for the advancement of the poor. It must never be forgotten that modern technology is the product of countries which are 'long' in capital and 'short' in labour, and that its main purpose, abundantly demonstrated by the trend towards automation, is to substitute machines for men. How could this technology fit the conditions of countries which suffer from a surplus of labour and a shortage of machines?

If we define the level of technology in terms of 'equipment cost per work-place', we can call the indigenous technology of a typical 'developing' country (symbolically speaking) a £1-technology, while that of the modern West could be called a £1,000-technology. The current attempt of the 'developing' countries, supported by foreign aid, to infiltrate the £1,000-technology into their economies inevitably kills off the £1-technology at an alarming rate, destroying traditional workplaces at a much faster rate than modern workplaces can be created and producing the 'dual economy' with its attendant evils of mass unemployment and mass migration. The gap between these two technologies is so enormous that a tolerably smooth transition from the one to the other is simply impossible, even if it were desirable.

It is obvious that the high average income of the developed countries derives primarily from the high level of capitalisation of the average workplace. But the development planners appear to overlook the equally obvious fact that such a high level of capital per workplace itself presupposes the existence of a high level of income. 'Income per man' and 'capital per workplace' stand in an organic relationship to each other, a relationship that can be 'stretched' to some extent—for instance with the help of foreign aid—but cannot be disregarded. The average annual income per worker and the average capital per workplace in the developed countries appear to stand in a relationship of roughly 1:1. This implies in general terms, that it takes one man-year to create one workplace, or that a man would have to save one month's earnings a year for twelve years to be able to buy his own workplace. If the relationship were 1:10, it would require ten man-years to create one workplace, and a man would have to save a month's earnings a year for 120 years, before he could make himself independent. This, of course, is an impossibility—and it follows that the £1,000-technology transplanted into a country the bulk of which is stuck on the level of a £1-technology simply cannot spread by any process of normal growth. It cannot have a positive 'demonstration effect'; on the contrary—as can be observed all over the world—its 'demonstration effect' is wholly negative. The vast majority of people, to whom the £1,000-technology is totally inaccessible, simply 'give up', while there remain small 'islands' of an alien world, which can in no way blend into the economy as a whole, and the extra income generated by these 'islands' is immediately absorbed by the cost arising from mass migration.

It is of course admitted that there are certain sectors and localities in every 'developing' country which are irrevocably committed to the employment of the most advanced technology in the world. In a typical 'developing' country these would account for perhaps 15 per cent of the population, and as there is no possibility of putting the clock back they will continue to exist. The question is what is to become of the other 85 per cent of the population. Simply to assume that the 'modern' sectors and localities will grow until they account for the whole is utterly unrealistic, for the reasons given. The task is to re-establish a healthy basis of existence for these other 85 per cent by means of an 'intermediate technology' which would be vastly superior in productivity to their traditional technology (in its present state of decay), while at the same time being vastly cheaper and simpler than the highly sophisticated and enormously capital-intensive technology of the West. As a general guide it may be said that this 'intermediate technology' should be on the level of £70-£100 equipment cost per average workplace. At this level, it would stand in a tolerably realistic relationship to the annual income obtainable by an able worker outside the westernised sectors.

These few indications must suffice, as space does not permit me to deal with the matter in the detail which it certainly would deserve. The question now to be considered is whether the development of such an 'intermediate technology' is realistically possible. It is unfortunately the case that many people are totally unable to imagine anything they are not already used to. There are countless development 'experts' who cannot even conceive the possibility of any industrial production unless all the paraphernalia of the Western way of life are provided in advance. The 'basis of everything', they say, is of course electricity, steel, cement, near-perfect organisation, sophisticated accountancy (preferably with computers), not to mention a most elaborate 'infrastructure' of transport and other public services worthy of an affluent society. Gigantic projects to provide this 'base' form the hard core of 'development plans' the world over. They are, of course, fairly easily arranged and carried out with the help of foreign aid and foreign contractors. This mentality, one is bound to insist, is perhaps the most destructive force operating in the 'developing' countries today. In the blind pursuit of an, in itself, highly questionable utopia, these 'experts' tend to neglect everything that is realistically possible. More than that, unfortunately: they denounce and ridicule every approach which relies on the employment and utilisation of humbler means.

It is none the less precisely in these humbler means that the only hope for real progress appears to lie. The countries counting as 'developed' today attained a fair level of general wealth long before the industrial revolution—a level far higher than that of the 'developing' countries today. They did this without electricity, steel, cement, computers, or an elaborate 'infrastructure'. Apart from the direct effects of war, pestilence, or occasional famines, they never had any appreciable part of their populations living in the kind of misery which is now the fate of countless millions the world over. Poverty, of course, has always been the lot of the majority of mankind: but misery, a helpless condition of utter degradation, as a permanent feature of life in town and country, associated with and promoted by the twin evils of unemployment and limitless urbanisation—this is a new phenomenon in the history of mankind, the direct result of modern technology thoughtlessly applied.

The 'intermediate technology' will not reject any, not even the most modern, devices, but it equally does not depend on them. It will use whatever is handy, insisting only on one thing: that the average equipment per workplace should not cost more than something of the order of £100. This is an average to be applied to every ordinary process of production, leaving out those special sectors, already mentioned, which are irrevocably committed to the Western way of life. On the basis of this stipulation any competent engineering firm can get to work and design the appropriate implements and methods to convert (mainly) local materials into useful goods for (mainly) local use. The types of industry to be tackled immediately would be:

(a) every kind of consumer goods industry, including building and building materials;

(b) agricultural implements;

(c) equipment for 'intermediate technology' industries.

It is only when, so to say, the circle is closed, so that, on the whole, the people are able to make their own tools and other equipment, that genuine economic development can take place. In a healthy society which employs an appropriate technology the argument that unemployment cannot be conquered for want of capital could never be true, because there would always be the possibility of turning unused labour to the production of capital goods.

Design studies for a small number of production processes on the suggested basis have already been made in India, with proper cost and price calculations. The results, as a matter of fact, are nothing short of sensational. The products of 'intermediate technology' are found to be fully competitive with those of Western technology. The modem prejudice that the best equipment is the best, irrespective of circumstances, is shown up—as might have been expected—as a gross error. It is the circumstances that decide what is best, and it is the principal task of every 'developing' country to apply a technology that is really appropriate to its circumstances. That a technology devised primarily for the purpose of saving labour should be inappropriate in a country troubled with a vast labour surplus could hardly be called surprising.

A remark of a general nature may be fitting at this point. It is generally assumed that the achievement of Western science, pure and applied, lies mainly in the apparatus and machinery that have been developed from it and that a rejection of the apparatus and machinery would be tantamount to a rejection of science. This is an excessively superficial view. The real achievement lies in the accumulation of knowledge of principles. These principles can be applied in a great variety of ways, of which the current application in Western industry is only one. The development of an 'intermediate technology', therefore, does not mean a return to an outdated system, something that is a mere 'second best'. On the contrary, it means a genuine forward movement into new territory. That some fundamental rethinking of the applications of modern science will be necessary before long is being recognised today even in the

West. There are many 'neuralgic points' which can already be identified without difficulty, where further technological developments
in the established direction are certain to produce 'negative
returns'—motor traffic in cities is merely the most obvious case in
point. Only slightly less obvious, albeit more controversial, is the
critical situation that may develop during the next twenty years or
so on account of the steep and accelerating rise in world energy
demands. 'Developing countries' which are committing themselves
in their forward thinking to the wholesale adoption of present-day
Western technology might do well to undertake a study of their
long-term energy needs and consider the likelihood or otherwise of
these needs being met.

Industrialisation as conceived by the majority of development
'experts' is in any case like a long, dark tunnel; they believe that a
marvellous light will be found at the end, no matter how long it
takes to reach it. But if energy supplies should become a limiting
factor, one might get stuck in the middle of the tunnel where it is
very dark indeed.

However that may be, the case for 'intermediate technology'
rests on the solid basis that there is no other means of fighting the
twin evils of mass unemployment and mass migration in the 'developing' countries. It also is the only way by which these countries
can achieve genuine economic independence and recover the kind
of social cohesion which the dual economy is in the process of
destroying. It should not be assumed that the development of
'intermediate technology' is a task of exceptional difficulty. On the
technical side, there exists already a wealth of useable material; but
it is extremely widely scattered and needs to be brought together.
In India, for instance, the Khadi Commission and a multitude of
other organisations have been working on this very subject,
although perhaps in a somewhat half-hearted way. The primary
lack, it would seem, has been of down-to-earth business sense. This
is not surprising, because in most cases the immediate need seemed
to be to protect and keep alive the activities of helpless people who,
without protection, would have become utterly destitute. The spirit of protection is rarely one conducive to enterprising business
management.

But the 'intermediate technology' is not in this sense protec-
tionist. It is not concerned with keeping alive activities which lack

essential viability: it is concerned with creating a new viability. The question has been raised whether this 'intermediate technology' is to be attained by upgrading the traditional technology or by down-grading Western technology. Either of these approaches may be feasible in some cases; but it is more likely that a new approach would be more promising: a new design derived from a sound knowledge of basic principles and conceived as a business venture. The kind of talent needed for this approach is available in many countries; the price of employing it would be merely a small frac-tion of the money now poured out on giant schemes which, even if successful, cannot lead to a real mitigation of the misery caused by mass unemployment and mass migration into cities.

Finally, a word might be said about raw material supplies. The 'intermediate technology' is of course far less sensitive to the qual-ity of raw materials than a more sophisticated technology. As men-tioned already, it will have to rely mainly on local materials, and these will be just the same as those on which all pre-industrial gen-erations have had to rely. It is a remarkable fact how much of the traditional knowledge of local materials has been lost during the last two or three generations. People will have to learn again that it is possible to have a highly productive agriculture by means of 'green manure' and other organic methods and that chemical fer-tilisers may not be the real answer at all. They will have to remem-ber how their forefathers built without modern cement and yet extremely durably; how much they relied on trees, not merely for the supply of food and materials but also for the improvement of soil and climate. With the help of modern knowledge they should now be able to do even better in these respects than their fore-fathers did. Tree planting, indeed, deserves to be singled out for special emphasis in this context, because the world is full of cases where the neglect of trees is one of the chief causes of misery and helplessness, while the recovery of a realistic sense of man's depen-dence on trees would be a most fruitful move in the right direction. No high technology or foreign aid is needed for planting and look-ing after trees; every able-bodied person can make his contribution and benefit from it; a wide range of useful materials can be obtained from trees—some species being very fast growers in tropical and semi-tropical climates—and these materials lend themselves exceptionally well for utilisation by 'intermediate technology'. Yet there are few 'developing' countries where trees do not suffer from heedless neglect. (To mention only one significant example, the half-term report on India's third five-year plan shows that it is precisely the planned activity in forestry which is most seriously behind schedule.) In most places there is no excuse for any alleged shortages of building materials. The planning experts should study how much has been built without modern cement throughout the ages.

The idea of 'intermediate technology', since it was formulated two years ago, has attracted a good deal of attention in many 'developing' countries. Highly important work has been done at the SET Institute at Hyderabad, and the Indian Planning Commission held a seminar on 'Intermediate Technologies' at that Institute in January, 1964. One of the papers submitted came from Professor D. R. Gadgil, the doyen of Indian economists, and some passages from it may form a fitting conclusion to this paper:

"Everything (he says) thus points to the desirability, nay, urgency, of initiating widespread industrial development in all regions of the country which will prevent accentuation of dualistic features within the economy and make for concerted and uniform economic progress. . . The scientists and the technicians must be made fully aware of what is expected out of the adoption of 'intermediate technology'. Their efforts must be directed towards the selection and development of those techniques which can serve the given aims. . . The process of evolving and adopting intermediate technology is a dynamic process which should be the centre of interest of the plan of industrialisation of the country. It should claim the attention, in an important way, of the ablest scientists and technicians in the country, and planning in relation to it should be undertaken through integrated planning of whole aspects and fields of industrial development."

Foreign aid will be fruitful, instead of destructive, only if it recognises these paramount needs and makes Western intellectual resources available to serve them. In closing, it might be mentioned that the United Kingdom is well placed to give assistance of the right kind. Its 'Rural Industries Bureau', for instance, established some forty years ago, may have only a minor role to play within the British economy, but it has a fund of accumulated experience (and literature) which could be invaluable for the 'developing' countries. Similar organisations exist in many other countries. What is immediately needed is a concerted effort of design.

Vol 1 No 2, July-Aug 1966

Chapter 14

Man Need Not Starve

THE WORLD FOOD PROBLEM has hit the headlines again, and rightly so. World population last year has risen by another seventy million, while world food production has remained stationary. The headlines talk about 'The World Hunger Gap—Shock Report', and the report in question, entitled *The State of Food and Agriculture, 1966*, comes from the Food and Agriculture Organisation of the United Nations. Its central message is that food availability per head of the world's population has fallen by two percent during last year. But this is not the crux of the story. Food production in the developing countries has dropped by four to five percent per head, and it is they who are really short. The fact that North American production has risen by about four percent and Western European production by one percent does little to improve the situation, except statistically.

Looking behind the surface of things, we find a dramatic change in the world food situation: the North American grain surpluses are running out. The large shipments of American grain to the developing countries did not come out of current production but out of stocks accumulated since the beginning of the 1950s. These stocks have now fallen to their lowest level in fourteen years; at fifteen million tons, they are said to be not enough for adequate protection against a domestic crop failure. *Time* reports in its issue of 12th August, 1966, that "the supply of soybeans, the dull yellow seed that goes into everything from vegetable oil to paint and constitutes the world's cheapest source of protein, equals just four months' consumption. Five years ago, Government warehouses were jammed with butter and cheese; now they have none. Washington has had to go into the market to buy dried milk for its program of free school lunches for 50 million children in 52 foreign countries."

In August 1966, the US State Department told American embassies that aid shipments of wheat would have to be cut by 25 percent, and Mr. Orville Freeman, the US Secretary for Agriculture, declared that "unless the hungry nations learn to feed themselves, there will be world famine in less than twenty years". He also said that "more human lives hang in the balance than have been lost in all the wars of history". If anything, he may have understated the seriousness of the situation by talking about the world as a whole. Food supplies do not and cannot 'average out'. The danger of famine in the developing countries is much nearer than "less than twenty years": it is here already. It is unlikely that there will be famine in North America, the Argentine, Australia, or the Soviet Union, or indeed in many smaller countries like Romania or Burma. No, the problem is much more concentrated than that and therefore much more urgent than world averages suggest.

The world food problem, of course, is closely allied to the world population problem; but here again it is not the rise in the total that is really significant. There are many countries, large and small, where further large increases in population will do no harm at all and may even be beneficial. What is really significant is that of the seventy million increase last year some fifty million accrued to the population of particular developing countries which are unable to cope. Neither people nor food will 'average out'.

Let us look at the proposition that 'food does not average out'. People say that it does not make sense to have restrictions on food production in America or Europe when there are starving millions in India. All right, if it does not make sense, can we get a more sensible world? By letting the North American plains produce food for India? This sounds simple enough, but how is India going to pay for it? If she cannot pay, the food has to go as aid. How, then, is the North American farmer to make a living? He would have to be paid by the American taxpayer through the American Government. Is this a feasible long-term proposition? I think not. In a short-term emergency, anything is possible and anything will do. But as a permanent way of life it seems to me to go against the most basic laws of human nature that the population in one part of the world should be maintained free of charge by the population in another part of the world. It is man's first task and duty to feed himself, either directly from his own soil or indirectly by way of trade.

Aid makes sense only if it is conducive to development, not if it merely supports a basically unsupportable situation. What should

ever come of such an arrangement? Do you think that permanent-
ly, as a matter of world planning, the Indians or the Egyptians or
whoever it might be could be pensioned off, as it were, to live on
the work and effort of the people of another nation? No man can
be free and maintain any kind of self-respect if he cannot even feed
himself, directly or indirectly. This, I think, is an unalterable law of
human nature, and we must dismiss from our minds any notion of
a world with food aid as a permanent feature.

It is interesting to look at the statistics on world food movements with these thoughts in mind. The most relevant food items are
grains because they are easily transportable in bulk. Before the war,
inter-continental grain shipments amounted to about twenty-four
million tons a year, and all of this went to Western Europe which
had the means to pay for it. In 1964/5, inter-continental grain shipments amounted to sixty million tons, a tremendous increase.
Europe took much the same as before, some twenty-four million
tons. New purchasers were the Soviet Union and China, taking a
similar amount and being able to pay for it. But a further amount
of over twenty million tons went to Asia and Africa as aid. Now
this aid food will progressively diminish and probably fade out
altogether. It had come out of stocks, and it seemed good business
to turn these stocks, if not into cash, at least into aid. As the stocks
disappear, so food aid will disappear and only trade will survive.
This is the new situation which the developing world will have to
face.

A certain inter-continental division of labour as between agriculture and industry will no doubt continue, and the rich countries
which cannot feed themselves from their own soil will continue to
be able to send industrial goods overseas so that overseas farmers
will produce food for them. But will the poor countries, the
so-called developing countries, be able to obtain significant
amounts of food in exchange for industrial exports? I should think
that to produce food for internal consumption will almost invariably be easier for a developing country than to produce industrial
products competitively for export, to pay for food imports. There
may be exceptions—there always are—but as a general proposition
this is an obvious truth. For many years to come, it will be utopian to think that arrangements could be made so that developing
countries could become large exporters of industrial goods to, say,

the United States, so as to be able to pay for large food imports from North America, or that they would make such exports to Europe, while Europe exported to America, so that American food could flow to the developing world. In short, Mr. Orville Freeman is undoubtedly right when he says that the hungry nations must learn to feed themselves. If they do not do so there may not be *world* hunger but *they* will starve, and this will not come to pass in twenty years but almost right away. Of course, this could have unpleasant effects on the countries—mainly Western Europe and Japan—which have for long been feeding themselves by trade. The "terms of trade" might change against them, so that they have to give more manufactured goods for their food imports: but there is no reason to fear that these countries will starve, because they are rich enough to pay. They have, moreover, the possibility to improve further upon their own agricultural performance, possibly to the point of self-sufficiency in food.

If this general line of argument is accepted, we can move on to the crucial question: *Can* the hungry nations feed themselves? Is it possible? Have they got enough land? Can they develop enough productivity? And here we come to a vital question: What do we mean when we say "productivity"? I know I am talking to a highly experienced audience and I apologise if the points I am going to make may seem too simple. It is often the most simple things that are most confused. When we talk of productivity in connection with the world food problem, the problem of hunger in developing countries, we are primarily talking about *productivity per acre* and not about *productivity per man*. Unless we keep this distinction constantly in mind we shall get everything mixed up. A given population with a given amount of land will have enough to eat if the output per acre is sufficient to feed them, irrespective of whether a quarter, or half, or 90 percent of the population are actually working on the land. If the output per acre is insufficient they will starve, even if the *productivity per man* is so high that only ten percent of the population are needed for work on the land.

Let us see, therefore, which countries have the highest agricultural productivity in terms of output per acre. To measure the overall productivity of land is a difficult business, and the best statistics available are probably those produced by the Food and Agriculture Organisation of the United Nations. Of the twelve countries shown with the highest productivity, per acre classified as agricultural land, in 1956-60, six were in Europe—the Netherlands, Belgium, Denmark, Federal Republic of Germany, Norway and Italy; three were in the Far East—Nationalist China (Taiwan), Japan, and Republic of Korea; two were in South East Asia—Malaya and Ceylon; and one in the Near East—the United Arab Republic [Egypt]. While statistics of this kind must not be taken too literally, they give valuable indications. It is interesting to note that the productivity per acre in the United Kingdom is shown as only one-half that of Germany, a third that of Belgium, and a quarter that of the United Arab Republic, and that that of the United States is shown as only about one-half that of the United Kingdom.

Now let us look at the other end of the scale, the dozen countries with the lowest overall productivity per acre. There are two of what used to be called the white dominions—Australia and South Africa; six countries in Latin America—Venezuela, Mexico, Argentine, Uruguay, Brazil, and Honduras; and four countries in Africa—Tunisia, Algeria, Morocco, and Ethiopia. The productivity gap between the "highest" and the "lowest" is as much as one to forty.

The ranking order of countries when it comes to productivity *per man,* i.e., per man engaged in agriculture, is of course entirely different. Whilst Australia has the lowest productivity per acre, its productivity per man is among the highest, and Korea, with its very high productivity per acre, is among the countries with the lowest productivity per man. There is no correlation between these two ranking orders, neither positive nor negative, for productivity per man correlates with the general wealth of the country, whereas productivity per acre correlates (if only to some extent) with the country's density of population.

All this goes to emphasise the importance of distinguishing these two measures of productivity— per acre and per man. As there is absolutely no positive correlation between them, you can imagine what confusion results when people fail to keep them apart.

One fact, at least, stands out: in a poor country a high output per acre is obtainable only through high labour intensity—see Korea, or Taiwan. This is hardly surprising, because *something* has to be applied to the land to make things grow, and if the country is poor it has little capital to apply to the land; it has only labour power. If it does not go in for labour-intensive cultivation, it will certainly not obtain high outputs per acre.

If we talk about the problem of hunger, as I said, we must talk primarily about productivity, or output, *per acre*. If we wished to discuss rural poverty we would have to talk about productivity, or output, *per man*. Hunger and poverty, although they often go together in towns, are easily distinguishable as regards the rural population. A lot of farmers and small cultivators in developing countries are desperately poor, but not necessarily hungry. It is often quite easy to increase the productivity *per man* at the expense of the productivity *per acre*. This may alleviate poverty but does nothing to solve the problem of hunger. It is often also quite easy to increase the output per acre at the expense of labour productivity. This helps to feed the hungry but does nothing to alleviate the poverty of the cultivators. The best, of course, is to raise both productivities, but where it is a matter of choice it must never be forgotten that the problem of hunger can yield only to an increase in the productivity per acre and is virtually unaffected by increases in the productivity per man.

Let us then turn to our central question: How can the hungry countries learn to feed themselves? It is indeed a matter of learning. Of all the factors that serve to improve agriculture, unquestionably the most important is *method*—the methods of good husbandry. To talk only of better seeds and better stock, of a better 'infrastructure' in the shape of roads and other facilities, or of the injection of more capital, is in my opinion to miss the decisive factor. To go even further and suggest that the 'hunger gap' could be closed by industrial type farming with high mechanisation, chemical fertilisers, insecticides, and so forth, is to become dangerously misleading.

If there is an answer to the problem of hunger in the developing countries, it can be found only in the principles of good husbandry. The spectre of hunger arises because in chasing after the unattainable people fail to attend to that which is within their reach. Countries with surplus populations on the land, largely underemployed or even unemployed, allow themselves to be enticed into the adoption of farming methods which are suitable for the wide open spaces of underpopulated continents or for highly industrialised communities with a shortage of agricultural labour. Countries desperately short of capital mechanise agriculture, substituting capital for men, adding to unemployment, and reducing the yield per acre. In general, most types of high mechanisation and most chemicals used on the land are labour-saving devices and as such quite inappropriate for poor countries with a large unemployment problem. There are of course exceptions—which merely prove the rule. Some land, if it is to be ploughed at all, must be ploughed very quickly, which can only be done by mechanised means. Some soils suffer from certain pronounced chemical deficiencies and cannot grow any proper crop at all unless these deficiencies are made good. But these exceptions must not blind us to the fact that high mechanisation and the use of chemicals in agriculture are primarily labour-saving devices which can add to output only on the assumption that the labour otherwise needed could not be made available.

I am very much aware that these statements may strike many of you as highly controversial. Since chemical fertilisers are for the soil a stimulant, they often have a striking short-run effect, and since they cause something like an addiction, their withdrawal can produce a sharp drop of yields. But this proves nothing. Comparisons have to be made with non-addicted soils and over long periods of time. Where these have been made, the results speak for themselves. In every case it emerges that good husbandry, methodical working with the maximum use of farm wastes, etc., produces long-run results which are as good, if not better, than those produced with the help of chemicals. And much the same applies also to modern pesticides, weed-killers, and so forth, all of them, some special cases apart, labour-saving devices.

Where labour is the bottleneck, let us by all means apply labour-saving devices. But where labour is in surplus and industrial products are scarce, it is bad economics to substitute the latter for the former, and to do so means to divert attention from the one thing needful—honest, good husbandry.

We are talking about the developing countries, countries in the grip of poverty, containing about two-thirds of the world's population and growing fast. The total world production of artificial fertilisers in 1961/63 amounted to about 35 million tons a year of which only 1.8 million tons, or 5 percent was produced in the developing countries. The Food and Agriculture Organisation has calculated that these countries should use 19 million tons by 1970 and 35 million tons by 1980—about thirteen years from now. I consider the attainment of such targets an absolute impossibility. But even if they could be attained, can millions, hundreds of millions of cultivators be taught to use them in a manner that does not hopelessly poison the soil? And if they can be taught, can they not equally, and probably more easily, be taught to adopt methods of good husbandry capable of achieving the same or even better results without artificial fertilisers? Experience shows that excellent farming with superlative yields per acre is possible and in fact being practised by individual farmers all over the world, without recourse to these costly products of industry. Where the methods are good, the yields are high, and where the methods are poor, slovenly and therefore wasteful, even artificial fertilisers do not produce good results. I wish the time would come when people would pay as much attention to a simple matter like farm accountancy in developing countries as they now devote to utopian dreams of educating a largely illiterate population in the intelligent use of dangerous materials like fertilisers, pesticides and so forth.

However that may be, one thing stands out: the hungry nations cannot get enough of these devices. They do not have the money to buy them and there is not enough aid available to let them have them free. It is no use telling them what they could do if they were already rich. A classic example of this kind of thinking can be found in the same issue of *Time* from which I have already quoted. I quote again:

> "If the short-range solution to hunger overseas is more United States food, the long-range answer must be the export of technology along with capital and brains to see that it is applied wisely. The rest of the world needs to catch up with the mechanisation and efficiency of U.S. farms. Half the world's tractors operate in North America. California rice growers have gone so far as to plant, fertilise and spray their crops entirely from planes. A single U.S. farm worker now feeds 37 people."

One wonders to whom this advice is directed. To Japan, or Italy, or Egypt, or Spain, where rice yields per acre are substantially higher than they are in the United States? Or to India, Pakistan and others, where the rice grower's income is so pitiful that he could not afford a bicycle, let alone a plane? But let me continue to quote:

> "Vital as research is, victory over hunger also demands that backward countries scale new heights of social, political and economic organisation. As the U.S. example shows, it takes vast amounts of capital—$30,500 per U.S. farm worker vs. $19,600 for an industrial worker . . . With carrot and stick, the U.S. now offers the underdeveloped world a chance—perhaps its last—to borrow U.S. techniques and reach for the same nourishing reward."

You might think it a bit unfair of me to quote such absurdities. Unfortunately, they are not untypical of what many people, even in high places, are thinking, saying, and doing. Just think of it: thirty thousand dollars per farm worker in India or Nigeria—so that he will then be able to feed 37 people, who will thereupon, no doubt, migrate into the big towns where they will find workplaces costing twenty thousand dollars each. This is their 'last chance'. In India alone some 200 million such workplaces will be needed, and at an average of twenty-five thousand dollars a piece, this will cost the trifling sum of five thousand milliard dollars— roughly 10,000 times as much as the yearly aid India is currently receiving from the United States. Marie Antoinette acquired an unenviable reputation for asking, on a certain occasion: "Why do these people shout for bread? Why don't they eat cake?" In comparison with these modern pundits, she must rank as an eminently sensible woman.

No doubt the poor must be given help, but within the harsh framework set by their poverty. No doubt the poor need technological aid, but at a level that is appropriate to their actual conditions. The fundamental cause of hunger and misery in the developing countries, and particularly in South East Asia, is not their backwardness but the condition of decay into which they have fallen. Not being an historian, I shall not attempt to analyse the historical causes. To-day, the decay is there for all to see. We speak of decay when people are doing badly that which they used to do well. Decay is not overcome by enticing them to do something entirely different, which they will do even more badly. It is not a matter of rejecting anything that is good, and even the most modern, most highly industrialised, and most sophisticated farming methods may have their occasional applicability in developing countries (assuming these methods are really sound in themselves). But there is a time scale which must not be overlooked. If we are thinking of the next thirty years, the period during which, according to authoritative estimates, world food production must treble if widespread hunger is to be avoided, it is certain that these ultra-modern methods will be merely a fringe phenomenon in the developing countries and that the question of Hunger will continue to be decided by hundreds of millions of humble peasants working their land along traditional lines. It is *their* decay that has to be overcome: it is *their* methods that have to be in some way upgraded and rationalised: it is they who have to be given a chance of using their labour power more fully and to better purpose, both in agricultural and in non-agricultural pursuits. The only way to fight hunger in the hungry countries is to involve the entire rural population in a kind of agricultural renaissance, in a process of true growth in which education and economic development go hand in hand.

Assume for a moment some sort of world government had at its disposal some twenty-five milliard dollars a year of aid funds, that is, perhaps three times the amount of aid currently being made available. At $25,000 a workplace, this aid could purchase a million new workplaces a year, whether in agriculture or industry. But at $250 per workplace, one hundred million workplaces could be newly created or substantially upgraded, and then we would start talking sense. For this is the relevant order of magnitude: a hundred million, not one million. In discussing the problem of world hunger we must talk of things capable of affecting hundreds of millions of peasants, otherwise we are wasting our time.

If, therefore, the capital endowment per workplace is screwed up to the level of modern technology, even the biggest conceivable aid programmes will not really touch the masses of peasants, the custodians of the soil on whose efforts everything depends. It follows that the real question is this: How can workplaces be upgraded, or newly created, with a capital expenditure of, say, $250 per workplace?

The twenty-five thousand dollar technology of the rich countries is readily available for anyone who is already rich; it is totally out of reach and therefore totally irrelevant for the poor peasants of this world. A two hundred and fifty dollar technology would mean something to them—in the context of aid—and it could reach a sufficient number of them to matter. Such a technology, which I have named 'Intermediate Technology', would be immensely more productive and more viable than the decayed traditional technology of those countries. It would, moreover, have the right educational impact, which is essential, for unless education and economic development go together there can be no genuine development at all.

The appropriate Intermediate Technologies already exist all over the world, even in the most highly developed countries, but they exist in an obscure and scattered way, so that the people who need them cannot find them. The whole process of aid tends to bypass them, it tends to offer the poor—with carrot and stick, as *Time* put it—the tools of the rich, which means that the poor get nothing at all and those already rich—who also exist in the poor countries—grow even richer. Officials, of course, tend to favour the glamorous technology, which is photogenic and something to boast about and raises no awkward questions of how to obtain the active participation of millions of people. But the price of this preference is a heavy one: a lack of real development and the prospect of world hunger.

Think of it—that in this year 1966 the Food and Agriculture Organisation of the United Nations tells us that the food availability per head in the developing countries is no greater today than it was in the 1930s, that food output has barely kept pace with the growth of population. But in the process the number of destitute people has vastly increased, while a wealthy minority has profited. Can this be called development? Is this the outcome of aid? Is it conceivable that human nature in the developing countries is so inadequate that this meagre result would not have been obtained even in the absence of aid? Is it possible that the aid giving has been largely futile? I do not know. Much of the aid effort has certainly been misconceived, which is not surprising, considering how difficult it is for the rich to understand the conditions of the poor. It is a tragic story, because there has been no lack of goodwill and genuine concern.

However that may be, even if we cannot solve the psychological problems, we can inject some new thinking into the debate on World Hunger and Economic Development by insisting that the technologies offered to the poor must be appropriate to the actual conditions of poverty, if they are to be of help. They must be Intermediate Technologies.

To promote these ideas—and to do something towards their implementation—a private, non-profit organisation has recently been set up in London under the name of Intermediate Technology Development Group Limited at 9 King Street, Covent Garden, London, WC2. One of the main purposes of the Group is to keep in intimate contact with industry, consulting engineers, and, of course, all aid-giving agencies. The response from industry has been magnificent and that from the developing countries, over-whelming. In all matters the Group tries to develop the 'basic approach'. Its slogans are 'Tools for Progress' and 'Education for Self-Help'. Now, what is the basic approach in agriculture?

In many developing countries, the most basic agricultural prob-lem is water. In the aid field, most of the thinking about water has been in terms of enormous dams and irrigation projects, costing millions of pounds. But the water is most needed exactly where it falls as rain, at the peasant's doorstep. If the peasant has to trek many miles to reach water, his position remains one of unalterable misery. The real task is to catch the water where it falls, in rain-water catchment tanks so designed that water will remain cool and protected and will neither seep away nor evaporate under the hot sun. A suitable technique has been devised by Mr. Michael Ionides by brilliantly combining the most ancient technique of water con-servation practised in the Sudan, with modern knowledge and materials. The result is a method which exactly fits the conditions of poor villagers who lack purchasing power but have a fairly ample supply of local labour. Every village should now be able to obtain a protected water supply, mainly by applying their own labour power.

The proper method has thus been developed, but to make it really available to the poor and needy, who are counted in hun-dreds of millions, two further steps, in my opinion, have to be taken. The method needs to be reduced, as it were, to a do-it-your-self kit, containing all required materials and the necessary instructions in a form which simple villagers can understand, and so proportioned that it easily fits on to a Land Rover. And there must be a big educational effort throughout the needy countries, using the existing primary school systems for the purpose. This would really be 'basic education', that is, an education designed to fit the pupil to live successfully in the actual conditions of his own country. It is only when these additional two steps are taken—two steps beyond the development of the method itself—that a real contribution to the problems of World Hunger and World Development will be made.

Let me give another example, very simple and down-to-earth. In many semi-arid regions the main occupation is cattle raising. The productivity—both per acre and per man—can be enormously increased by controlled grazing, which however normally requires extensive fencing. What is the cost of fencing in Africa? People open a drawer full of quotations from the developed countries, and the answer is "£100 a mile". At this cost, it is obvious, extensive fencing is utterly beyond the reach of poor villagers. This problem still awaits its Michael Ionides. I hope the Intermediate Technology Development Group will tackle it. We need a really low-cost method of fencing, with a maximum use of local labour and a minimum use of in-bought materials, and that method 'reduced' to a do-it-yourself kit to fit on to a Land Rover. And then everybody who needs it must somehow be told about it and have a chance of acquiring the know-how.

Countless other examples could be given. High on the priority list must be the problem of crop storage. It is a matter of pretty well established fact that the poorest countries suffer the greatest losses—often thirty to forty percent of the harvest—because of lack of proper storage. Yet I doubt that there is an insufficiency of knowledge and experience on how to store safely. Only, the existing knowledge does not reach those who need it most; it has not been 'reduced' to a do-it-yourself kit and has not been introduced into the primary school curriculum—if you will allow me this slightly symbolical way of expressing myself. The same basic approach has to be applied to every form of building, bridging, transport, and processing and other production in rural areas, with the invariable objective of minimising the need for inbought materials and thus enabling the poor peasants to utilise their one major asset, their own labour power, but on a much higher level of productivity and viability than is common at present.

I believe that the problem of World Hunger can be solved along these lines and *along these lines only*. At the risk of repeating myself I emphasise that the poor peasants are the custodians of the soil in the hungry countries and that it is the poor peasants and no one else who will, or will not, double and treble the productivity of their acres, as is required if famine is to be avoided. Food is produced in rural areas, not in the big cities. Food surpluses from the rural areas are needed to feed the ever-growing cities. The central economic task of mankind, at this juncture, is to build up an efficient and satisfactory way of life in the rural areas, to achieve an agro-industrial structure which conquers unemployment, stops rural decay, and arrests the seemingly irresistible drift of destitute people from the countryside into the big cities, already overcrowded and rapidly becoming unmanageable.

The world food problem is not primarily a *scientific* problem. It is a problem of mass mobilisation, of mass education towards 'the next step' of making available the appropriate technologies to hundreds of millions of peasants. Needless to say, in many countries it is also a political problem—but this aspect goes beyond my present terms of reference.

It should be abundantly clear from what I have said that Factory Farming can have no relevance whatever to the question of avoiding famine in the hungry countries. What happens in the Factory Farm is not primary production, but secondary production: a process of conversion, like turning coal into electricity. No one, surely, makes the mistake of the dear old lady who after seeing a film about the tough life of coal miners exclaimed: "I shall never again burn coal, but immediately switch over to electricity!" When coal is burned to make electricity, about seventy percent of the calories contained in the coal are lost. When feeding stuffs are turned into poultry or veal in Factory Farms some eighty to eighty-five percent of the calories contained in the feeding stuffs are lost. This conversion, therefore, can have nothing to do with feeding the hungry.

It is also easy to see that the main *raison d'être* of Factory Farming is to save human labour. Whether it ultimately achieves even this, may be doubtful; I am not qualified to judge it. What is certain is that the impulsion towards labour-saving does not

reasonably exist in the hungry countries which suffer from a surplus of labour and a shortage of capital.

A final point about Factory Farming in the developing countries
is worth making. Perhaps the greatest problem of these countries is
the problem of alienation, of being faced with so much that is
strange and incomprehensible and incompatible with tradition that
the ordinary people become bewildered and timid, while the educated lose contact with the ordinary people. And what more terrible method of alienation could be devised than a type of farming
that alienated even the animals from their natural life and induced
man to treat them in a manner utterly irreconcilable with the simplest teachings of religion ?

For a man to put himself into a wrongful relationship with animals and particularly those long domesticated by him, has always
been considered a horrible and infinitely dangerous thing to do.
There have been no holy men in our history or in anybody else's
history who were cruel to animals, and innumerable are the stories
and legends which link sanctity with a loving kindness towards
lower creation. In *Proverbs* we read that the just man takes care of
his beast, but the heart of the wicked is merciless, and St. Thomas
Aquinas wrote: "It is evident that if a man practises a compassionate affection for animals, he is all the more disposed to feel compassion for his fellow men." And I might also quote Pope Pius XII
who said: "The animal world, as all creation, is a manifestation of
God's power, his wisdom, and his goodness, and as such deserves
man's respect and consideration. Any reckless desire to kill off animals, all unnecessary harshness and callous cruelty toward them is
to be condemned. Such conduct, moreover, is baneful to a healthy
human sentiment and only tends to brutalise it."

Have the sayings of the saints and sages anything to do with the
practical problem of feeding the hungry? Yes. Man does not live by
bread alone and if he thinks he can disregard this truth and can
allow the 'human sentiment' to become brutalised, he does not lose
his technical intelligence but his power of sound judgement, with
the result that even the bread fails him—in one way or another.
Another way of putting the same thing is this: Man's greatest single task today is to develop in himself the power of non-violence.
Everything he does violently, for instance in agriculture, could also
be done relatively non-violently, that is, gently, organically, patiently

adapted to the rhythms of life. The true task of all further research and development is surely to devise non-violent methods of reaching the results which man requires for his existence on earth. The violent methods always seem to produce bigger results more quickly; in fact, they lead to the accumulation of insoluble problems, particularly with the World Food Problem. But there is a way, a non-violent way. It is based on a true compassion for hundreds of millions of humble peasants throughout the world and an effort of the imagination to recognise the boundaries of their poverty. It leads to policies that truly help them to help themselves. This is the way we must seek. It is humane, democratic and, I can assure you, surprisingly cheap.

Vol 1 No 10, Nov-Dec 1967

CITIES & THE LAND

Chapter 15

No Future for Megapolis

MODERN URBANISATION, as we all know, is a very recent thing. Although the first cities arose some 5,000 to 6,000 years ago, the kind of metropolis or megalopolis which we now accept as 'normal' is a good deal less than a hundred years old.

Kingsley Davis, one of the best known students of the subject, said a few years ago: "Clearly the world as a whole is not fully urbanised, but it soon will be." One may wonder on what he bases this prediction. I suspect it is based on little more than past and current trends. As a statistician, I am never happy with the extrapolation of trends, unless I can get some understanding of what lies behind the trends themselves, what has made them possible and what keeps them going. Kingsley Davis holds that "urbanised societies, in which a majority of the people live crowded together in towns and cities, represent a new and fundamental step in man's social evolution". I do not know whether he means to offer this thought as an explanation of the past hundred years, during which this "new and fundamental step" was taken in so many parts of the world, or as a justification for his assumption that full urbanisation of the world as a whole will soon be implemented. The idea of a new and fundamental step in human social evolution seems to suggest something which, once accomplished, will stay for good. But here lies the very question: Why did it happen? What are the forces that have made it happen? What is the material basis of this happening, and is this material basis permanent or perhaps impermanent? The idea of evolution may be a useful way of describing the past, but rarely serves to explain it, and when it comes to the future its predictive value is more than doubtful.

To obtain another view of this astonishing phenomenon—a majority of the people crowding together in towns and cities—we might remind ourselves of the well-known fact that seventy percent of the citizens of the United States, and comparable proportions in other industrial countries, live in cities occupying little over one percent of the total land space. This gives some idea of the degree of concentration. "The large and dense agglomerations comprising the urban population," says Kingsley Davis, ". . .exceed in size the communities of any other large animal; they suggest the behaviour of communal insects rather than of mammals." For mammals to behave like communal insects may be described as a new and fundamental step in their social evolution, but it is not immediately apparent that it is a step in the right direction.

Towns and cities consist of a huge variety of more or less permanent structures, and that is why it cannot be a waste of time for those responsible for these structures to give some thought to the kind of questions I have raised. What is the relevant 'time horizon'? Buildings made of stone or concrete are not erected with the idea of early destruction. If they are to stand up at all, their basic structure must be sound, and if they are able to stand up for ten years, there is no reason to believe that they cannot equally well stand up for a hundred years and even a lot more, given a reasonable amount of care and maintenance. If I were an architect, this thought, I suspect, would worry me, even to the point of paralysis, which is no doubt a sufficient reason for my not having become an architect. Doctors and surgeons, to give an obvious example, are in an easier position. Their worst mistakes are quickly buried. But the mistakes of architects remain in the fullest evidence for countless generations!

All I wish to point out, or rather to recall to mind, is that the relevant 'time horizon' for anyone concerned with permanent structures is formidably long. These structures do not merely have to 'fit' today; they have to continue to be 'fitting' for a very long time. Some civilisations have drawn the conclusion that they could not take it upon themselves to enter, as it were, a commitment for an indefinite, and possibly very long period; so they used only such building materials as were subject to a 'normal' rate of decay: wood, bamboo sticks, or even paper. Other civilisations, like medieval Europe, drew the conclusion that buildings, being 'of the nature of eternity', could and should not be subjected to the economic calculus, like other human artifacts: only the best would be good enough; only something worthy of being dedicated to the glory of God would be worthy of the dignity of human beings. And if this aspiration could not be fulfilled in all cases, it was certainly fulfilled with regard to the great majority of prominent buildings. Our civilisation disposes of building materials of a truly awe-inspiring durability. Some of the bomb shelters built for what was happily thought of as a strictly temporary emergency during the last war, are of such indestructibility that the cost of demolishing them is something no one can face: so we leave them standing in all their hideous glory.

To return to our starting point: urbanisation in the modern sense is a very recent phenomenon, less than a hundred years old. If it had been possible before, why did it not happen? If it had been impossible before, what was it that made it possible? These, I suggest, are the two questions, to which we must turn our attention. I think there is plenty of historical evidence that important cities, Rome, for instance, have tended to grow and grow, until they could grow no further. What was it that stopped their growth? The answer is simple: they could not be provisioned any more. They lived on their surroundings, and as they became bigger they had to be provisioned from ever more extended surroundings; and as distances had to extend, transport could no longer cope. The bottleneck was transport, and the bottleneck of transport was energy. Human and animal power cannot manage long distances, except for imperishable goods, and even when it does manage them it becomes, at a certain point intolerably expensive.

During the nineteenth century, Western society broke through this barrier by learning to exploit nature's storehouse of fossil fuels, first coal, then oil. Coal led to rail transport, because it is rather crude and heavy and therefore best used in locomotives pulling a large number of coaches or trucks; while oil led to motor transport because it is subtle, easily divisible, of high calorific value per unit of volume as well as per unit of weight, and therefore ideally suited for fast, small-scale, decentralised transport from any point to any other point, provided only there is some kind of a road. The exploitation of fossil fuels was the primary factor, while the flowering of technical ingenuity was a secondary factor, because, in a certain sense, the material, in this material world, is the indispensable basis of the intellectual.

The development of large-scale urbanisation, as we have witnessed it over the last hundred years, required the intervention of a further factor: How could people leave the land and crowd together in towns and cities, and still get fed? The limiting factor on urbanisation is the productivity of agriculture, and the meaning of 'productivity' in this context is output-per-person rather than output-per-acre. Towns and cities exist on the agricultural surplus of the countryside; pure subsistence farming cannot sustain even the smallest degree of urbanisation. How, then, has it been possible to sustain the high degree of urbanisation which has occurred during the last hundred years? By an immense improvement of the productivity-per-person in modern agriculture. Fewer and fewer people were required to till the soil, with the result that more and more people could leave the soil and go into cities.

Every answer tends to lead to a further question, and our next question must be this: How has this stupendous and historically unparalleled increase of productivity per-person in agriculture been achieved? The most important single factor has been the introduction of new technologies based on fossil fuels. Modern agricultural technology, as practised in the United States, in Western Europe, in the areas affected by the 'green revolution', and in many other parts of the world, is essentially oil-based. Its tremendous success in raising productivity-per-person was achieved by the introduction of an intensely oil-based technology, intensive mechanisation and, even more importantly, intensive chemicalisation. In terms of physics and chemistry, modern society eats a variety of foodstuffs but in terms of economics, it eats oil.

If the modern type of urbanisation has not been possible before, roughly speaking, the middle of the nineteenth century, what was it that made it possible? The answer is threefold: the exploitation of nature's storehouse of fossil fuels, the development of a highly efficient transport system, initially coal-based but now primarily oil-based, the development of agricultural technologies which are virtually dependent on oil.

Until a few years ago, we took oil for granted. In the autumn of 1967, for instance, the then Minister of Power presented a White Paper to Parliament, entitled 'Fuel Policy'. Its central message was this: "Subject to overriding considerations of adequacy and security of supplies, the Government's basic objective can be summarised as cheap energy. . . What is important is that we should take full advantage of the cheapness and technical merit of nuclear power, North Sea gas, and oil." The Minister had no real doubts about the adequacy and security of oil supplies and therefore mapped out the further contraction of the British coal industry, the speed of which, however, would have to be controlled so as to avoid undue hardship to coal miners and their communities. In a sagacious paragraph he dealt with future oil costs. "It is difficult to predict the course of oil prices. There are a number of reasons for expecting them not to increase. The industry is continually searching for ways of cutting costs, as for instance by the use of very large crude oil tankers to reduce freight charges and increase flexibility and security of supply, and the surplus of crude oil seems likely to persist for many years despite the expansion in world demand. Here and elsewhere oil will be up against increasingly strong competition from natural gas and nuclear power. On the evidence available, it seems likely that oil will remain competitive with coal, and that pressure to force up crude oil prices will be held in check by the danger of loss of markets."

These sanguine arguments did not go unchallenged, but no one was willing to listen to the challengers, because the enticing dream of 'cheap fuel for ever' kept everybody happy. We now have a very rude awakening. The following official figures makes the point: in 1970, our average monthly crude oil imports amounted to 8.3 million tons; at an average value per ton of £4.80, these monthly imports cost the country £40 million. In March 1974, our crude oil imports were rather high at 9.6 million tons; the average value per ton was £28.9, and the total bill came to £278 million; compared with four years ago, an increased burden on our balance of payments of nearly £240 million a month.

Pressure to force up crude oil prices, we had been told, would be held in check by the danger of loss of markets. Do you think the oil exporting countries are worried about a loss of markets when the export of one ton of crude oil produces for them an amount of money which, only four years ago, required the export of six tons? On the contrary, they would rejoice in the loss of markets, if only they could see it happening. They have been pleading for years that the oil importing countries should reduce their requirements. From their point of view, a loss of markets is the very thing they have been longing for ever since they realised, some ten years ago, that their own proved oil reserves were by no means infinite and would be exhausted in a matter of twenty or thirty years if they 'maintained their markets'. In ever more insistent tones they have pleaded: "Please mitigate your requirements; if we sell all we have got within twenty or thirty years, what is to become of us? We cannot build up an alternative livelihood for our peoples within two or three decades."

On the sixth of October 1973, the outbreak of yet another Arab-Israeli war provided the historical opportunity for the Arabian oil exporting countries to establish a radically new situation as regards crude oil prices. Within a few months, these prices quadrupled, and their fundamental aim, which is to conserve their proven oil reserves to last longer than a mere twenty or thirty years, can now be attained via the so-called price mechanism. We hear nothing more about using oil as a political weapon; what we shall be hearing more and more insistently from now on is this: "Of course, you can buy all the oil you want, but how are you going to pay for it?" And the truth of the matter is that we cannot pay for the amount of imported oil which our economies have got used to.

Whether the crunch will come within three months or three years is hard to predict. But, I suggest, nothing of any real importance hinges on precision in these matters, certainly not for builders, architects, town planners and such like, whose 'time horizon' is counted in decades, if not centuries. That the days of the cheap-fuel economy are counted, in fact that they are over, there cannot be any reasonable doubt. The sooner we realise and accept this, the better will be our chance of adjusting to the new situation without having to go through a period of unimaginable troubles.

The effects of a hundred years of cheapness-and-plenty as regards fossil fuels have been extraordinarily far-reaching. The effects of the coming period of dearness-and-scarcity as regards fossil fuels, not necessarily in all parts of the world, but inescapably in Western Europe, Japan, and many of the so-called developing countries, will be equally far-reaching.

The cheapness and plenty of fossil fuels also led to the large-scale production of highly fuel-intensive building materials, such as cement and steel; to building methods characterised by the substitution of fuel-intensive mechanisation for human labour; and to the erection of buildings such as high-rise flats, hotels, and office blocks, which in themselves are, as it were, engines dependent for their functioning on a continuous high rate of fuel consumption.

If cheapness-and-plenty, as regards fuel, has produced these effects, what is going to be the effect of dearness-and-scarcity? This is the crucial question. It is a question of such overwhelming magnitude that we have to give ourselves a very big push to be prepared to look it in the face. It is much easier to shut one's eyes and go on dreaming; to divert attention to such questions as: "How do you propose to persuade people to change their life-style?" or: "Are you sure that people want change?", and to engage in endless debates on possible alterations of the 'political system', etc. I am not suggesting that these and similar questions are completely irrelevant, but they are of a secondary nature: in future the tune will be called by fuel supplies, and not primarily by our likes and dislikes. Even if the great majority of people had a strong preference for crowding together in huge cities, the fact remains that high-density living patterns can be sustained only by high-density fuels. If the availability of the latter is called into question the possibility of the former is called into question. In other words, far from accepting Kingsley Davis' prediction that the whole world will soon be 'fully urbanised' we have now to consider the possibility that some of the most highly urbanised parts of the world, such as Western Europe and Japan, may have to find ways of achieving some degree of de-urbanisation: because, if high-density fuels become very expensive and hard to obtain, high-density living becomes increasingly unsupportable.

The modern system of agriculture is obviously extremely vulnerable to adverse changes on the oil front. We can see this already to-day as we witness the virtual collapse of the 'Green Revolution' in a number of developing countries. It has been calculated how much oil would be required if the whole world, some 4,000 million people, forgetting any further increases in world population, were to be fed by means of modern agricultural technology. The answer is that on such assumptions all proved oil reserves, as currently known, would be exhausted by agriculture alone within less than thirty years. It would seem to follow that the modern system of agriculture has no long-term future, and that there is a somewhat urgent need for the development of alternative systems, systems much less oil-intensive. The answer one normally obtains to such a proposition is that these alternatives, even if they were possible, would be relatively much more labour-intensive than the modern systems. In other words, the proportion of people working the land would have to rise, which means that the proportion of people living and working in cities would have to fall.

It is precisely this possibility, or rather this possible necessity, that ought to engage our most serious attention. If more people are going to be needed in agriculture, it will be necessary to upgrade and redevelop the life of rural communities. This is a very tall order. For more than a century, all the emphasis has been on city-life, and the brain-drain at the expense of the rural areas has been devastatingly severe. To reverse the century-old trend will not be easy, but neither will it be impossible. There are many signs among the young that a push of necessity in this direction might even be welcomed.

Turning now to transport, we find a rather similar picture. Cheap and fast transport has made modern urbanisation possible. Mobility is thought of as a very great value, and this value-judgement has been sustained by the availability of cheap and plentiful oil. If the forward estimates of so-called transport requirements which underlie, for instance, the Channel Tunnel project are to be taken seriously, we shall need to devote at least two or three times as much oil to transport in twenty years time as we do now. These estimates stem from an historical situation which is now gone and unlikely ever to return. The new situation demands that we should ask ourselves: 'Why do we seem to need so much transport?' What is it in our patterns of production, our patterns of consumption, our distribution of population, in short, what is it in our life-style that entails such enormous and ever-increasing transport requirements? After all, the goods we shift about do not become better by being shifted about. Why is it that they appear to become more valuable?

Production patterns that give primary emphasis to mechanisation and automation tend to get burdened with very high overhead costs, and it then appears to be 'economical' to let the product invade faraway markets, even if the net return on such sales yields less than average revenue: it still helps to 'spread overheads'. Very large mass-production units obviously entail a very large commitment to massive long-distance transport. Economists claim that this enlarges consumers' choice; but they generally do not mention that it reduces the chance of consumers of choosing locations that are free from intolerable traffic noise and contaminated air.

In future, transport planning needs to concern itself with much more than transport: its principal aim will be the reduction of transport requirements, which have grown beyond all reasonable bounds. In other words, it will become increasingly desirable to bring production and consumption much more closely together. The present pattern with cars being produced in Tokyo in order to be used in Coventry, does not seem to be the most rational human ingenuity can devise, and it would assuredly not be improved if the transport of cars from Tokyo to Coventry were made faster or even cheaper by some fantastic technological breakthrough.

Not only the pattern of production, but also the pattern of consumption will have to change. Already there are reports of significant numbers of high-rise hotels in Mediterranean holiday resorts being unable to open for the summer season. What is to become of innumerable blocks of high-rise flats, once the remorseless increase in energy costs has worked its way through the system, heaven only knows. Solar energy and wind power can do little to reduce their dependence on fossil fuels.

However, I do not wish to dwell on the future of buildings already erected. What about buildings to be erected in the future? The change in the fuel situation from cheapness-and-plenty to dearness-and-scarcity calls for new types of calculation and new criteria of efficiency. Needless to say, everything calculable in terms of money will have to continue being calculated in money, but most of these money calculations will have to be supplemented and checked against calculations made in terms of fuel units, such as calories. We may not be able to afford things which are expensive in terms of calories, even if they appear to be relatively cheap in terms of money. Here again, I cannot go into detail. At present, there is still a great deal of talk about 'alternative sources of energy', and most people imagine that, although fuel may become very much more expensive, there is enough of it somewhere in the world for it never to become scarce. What they fail to realise is that there is not only a money cost of fuel but also a fuel cost of fuel. The Bureau of Mines in the United States has recently begun a study to determine how many calories it takes to produce various types of fuels: what matters is not the gross energy production, but the net energy gain. Professor Odum of the University of Florida says "the biggest lesson to be learned from net-energy thinking is that all the new technologies being developed to attain energy independence are draining present energy supplies and are therefore hastening the day when fossil fuels run out. For example, enriching uranium for light-water reactors consumes, in the form of coal, 60% of the energy released from the nuclear fuel." Whether any nuclear energy producer is, in fact, a net energy producer at all, is still very much an open question.

The life-style of the modern world is characterised by a very high rate of what we might call economic metabolism, that is to say, an enormous throughput of resources to obtain a standard of living which still is, for most people, deplorably low. In a strange and paradoxical way, we have to run faster and faster merely to stand still. Although the economic metabolic rate of the average American is something like fifty times as high as that of the average Indian, and that of the average Western European about thirty times as high, the rich societies of the world are pursuing the struggle for further metabolic growth with even greater single-mindedness than the poor. Yet such further growth as is being achieved does not seem to lighten the burden of existence but, on the contrary, to increase it. If fuel and material shortages should make further growth impossible or even enforce the reduction of certain activities, people fear that nothing but misery can be in store for them.

All this stems from a confusion of thought which takes the metabolic rate for the equivalent of the standard of living. Is our standard of living really determined by the rate at which we manage to consume, that is to say: to destroy and use up, valuable goods and services? We know families who consume very much and live very badly: both husband and wife have to go out to work; they return from work exhausted and disgruntled and have no strength left in them for anything but watching television; the children feel neglected and present their parents with endless problems which are as insoluble as they are costly to cope with; expensive holidays fail to undo the damage done during the rest of the year, etcetera. Yet we also know families who consume relatively very little and live rather well. How do they do it? The rate of metabolism, economically speaking, of the former is high; that of the latter is low. Whose is the higher standard of living?

A neat little prescription that is often given is: 'Cycle and re-cycle'. Cycling, of course, is a mode of transportation with a delightfully low rate of economic metabolism. The cyclist's rate of physiological metabolism is somewhat higher than that of the motorist; but that can save him, or society, a lot of doctor's bills! Re-cycling, on the other hand, desirable as it often may be, fails to go to the root of the matter. Why tolerate a high rate of waste and then try to cope with the problem by re-cycling? Would it not be more intelligent first of all to try and reduce the rate of waste? The re-cycling problem may then itself become much more manageable.

We might do well to distinguish between permanent goods on the one hand and ephemeral goods on the other. A life-style which puts primary emphasis on the consumption of ephemeral goods and services requires an economic system with a high rate of metabolism and therefore creates innumerable problems of pollution, tends to ruin the environment, and inevitably runs up against severe resource bottlenecks. Now, of course, a certain flow of ephemeral goods, to be destroyed in the act of consumption, is indispensable for human life; but it might be wise to keep this flow at a modest level and to put the main emphasis on the creation of permanent goods, that is to say, lasting improvements of the environment, excellent tools and equipment, health of soil, plants, animals and people, work opportunities which can be genuinely enjoyed, and even beautiful buildings, villages, and towns, together with beautiful things to be put into buildings, villages, and towns. Such a life-style would not require an economic system with an unsupportably high rate of metabolism, yet there would be no smell of misery and degradation about it.

I believe that great pressures upon human nature will be exerted by the logic of facts which will make our present lifestyle increasingly difficult to sustain. We can meet these pressures with calm forethought and give them a creative response. If we do that, why should we despair of the future of our civilisation even if we have to lower our rate of economic metabolism? Why should we refuse to believe that, endowed with so much more scientific knowledge and technical ability than any previous generation, we should be able to build a much more satisfactory life than we have ever known?

Vol 5 No 6, Jan-Feb 1975

The Use of the Land

THE SUBJECT OF THE PROPER USE OF LAND at first sight looks some-what technical, but the more I think about it the more I realise it is not; it is a highly philosophical subject and we are really deceiving ourselves if we think that it requires a special inventiveness of a technical kind to cope with the problems of land use.

There are always some things which we do for their own sakes, and then there are other things which we do for some other purpose. One of the most important tasks for any society is to distinguish between ends and means and to have some sort of cohesive view and some sort of an agreement about this. What are the things we do for their own sake, and what are the things which we do for a purpose other than themselves?

Now, anything that we do for its own sake does not lend itself to calculation. For instance, most of us try to keep ourselves reasonably clean. You cannot calculate the value of this; certainly you cannot apply an economic calculus. In fact, to wash is totally un-economic. Nobody has ever made any profit out of washing himself. There are many activities, when you come to think of it, which are totally uneconomic because they are carried on for their own sakes. So the first point I am making is that ends, as distinct from means are not matters of economic calculation. They are not economic but, if you like, meta-economic. Just as we can have physics and meta-physics, so we can have economics and meta-economics.

What are the big meta-economic factors? I think one is brought back to the four elements that the ancients used to talk about—air, water, earth and fire. These are meta-economic factors. We have not made them, but we depend on them: on each of those four basic elements. They are worth looking after, not as means to an end but as ends in themselves. We do not ask today whether it is economic to take some care to have clean air. No, we say this is a good thing in itself. We can argue that if we neglect it we might suffer, but this is not an economic argument. We want clean air as a value in itself. The same about water; the same as I am trying to tell my contemporaries, about the basic energy resources, the element fire. And today we are talking about land, the element earth. I should say that land presents a problem of meta-economics; but let us realise we do not have a consensus of opinion on this point in present-day society.

People believe today that clean air and clean water are worthy objectives but is land to be considered as an end in itself worth bothering about? I am afraid we are still a long way from that. Of course, it can still come; you only have to think back about 100 years when many people were quite incapable of thinking of the fifth element as an end in itself, which is of course the human being—man himself. We had theories, which are still leading a ghostly and unpleasant existence, that man was just an economic phenomenon. His income, for instance, should be settled by market forces. Whether he had the chance to work or not should be settled by whether or not the whole economy was easier to manage at this level or that level of employment. All this used to be considered merely sound, scientific sense. But I am glad to say we have to some extent got away from this; in present-day economics man is generally taken not as a means to an end but as an end in itself. You know what happens when people start mixing up means and ends. The fellow who goes on earning money and forgets that money is only a means to an end comes in for ridicule and contempt as a miser, an unsavoury sort of character. All the same, you find all through present day societies all sorts of extraordinary attempts to reduce what we all recognise as final values to an economic calculus.

People ask, "Does education really pay off?", as if a monetary return were the purpose of education; as if education were not a value in itself. Some people ask whether crime pays, and that is a legitimate question. But if they ask, "Does goodness pay? Is it worthwhile? Is it good business to behave decently?", we immediately realise, although perhaps we cannot find the argument against it, that this is an illegitimate, a degraded question. So I am saying that if one mistakes what is an end in itself, and treats it as a means, then there is a degradation of life. And conversely, if one takes what is really a means to be an end and elevates it to the status of an end, then there is degradation of oneself. Like the example of the miser.

So now we come to our question: Can we say, do we believe, that a healthy and beautiful countryside is an end in itself? The moment we say yes to that, we do not have to discuss any more whether it is economic or uneconomic, just as we do not have to discuss whether to keep reasonably clean is economic or uneconomic. We say cleanliness is an end in itself and any self-respecting people would agree. That is why I say the problem of land use is not primarily an economic or technical question.

The problem is confused, however, by the fact that one can buy and sell land as if it were simply a man-made thing. Luckily we cannot buy and sell the air, and this helps people to understand that clean air is an end in itself. But because one can buy and sell land they tend to think that land is just the same as a pair of nylon stockings, or a glass of beer, or any other secondary product — something you buy and sell. If this were true, we would have nothing to discuss, because if there is nothing more to it than that, then the economic calculus must indeed be given full control.

We waste our time if we think this is a matter for scientific proof. No one can prove that it is right to love anybody, or to care for anything, or to have respect for anything. No one can prove that it is right to care for the future. If somebody says to me "Thou shalt not exploit thy fellow man," I can always answer "Why not?"; "Thou shalt not kill"—"Why not?" There is no conclusion to it in logic. We see intuitively—call it what you like—that there are values that do not have to be argued, with regard to not exploiting or killing our fellow men. In the same way, do we or do we not accept that land, the use, maintenance, health and future of land is one of these values?

If I have a car, I can quite legitimately argue that the best way to use it is never to bother about maintenance and simply run it to ruin. I may indeed have calculated that this is the best, the most economical method of use. If the calculation is correct, nobody can criticise me for it: there is nothing holy about a car. A car is simply a means to an end, and if this end is best achieved by not bothering about maintenance, and so on, but just running the car to ruin, that's fine. Is land the same sort of thing as a car, or is it a different thing? That is the whole question.

Equally, what about the creatures on the land, the higher animals? Are they the same as a car, a mere utility? Or are they also to be looked upon as values in themselves? Now, again, this is a perfectly straightforward question. Modern zoologists and biologists can tell us the most entrancing stories about these animals, which make it clear to anyone who cannot see it directly, that every animal is a mystery far beyond our comprehension. They show us with all the armoury of science, for instance, that among the higher animals most of the inner organs are very similar. But outwardly there are breathtaking differences—antlers, horns and many other magnificent signs that go far beyond any utilitarian calculus. Where utility is the decisive thing, the zoologist tells us, all organs are much the same. But where something else comes into it, whatever that might be—the symbolism, the hint towards something higher than humdrum life—there we encounter a vast display of ingenuity and beauty. Well, are we going to accept this and say here are values in themselves, or are we going to say an animal is just the same as a car?

I know some people think that a car is much more beautiful than a bull. But there is no use arguing about it; either you see something or you don't! Perhaps it is more a matter of faith than of anything else; it certainly is not a matter of logic.

In the past, of course, things were different. We were told to value the things which we certainly had not made ourselves, because God made them and had found them "very good". But today we live in an irreligious, not to say anti-religious society, and an argument involving God cuts no ice at all. We are therefore reduced to a different type of argument, namely, the threat, "Look here, if you do not behave yourself, you will regret it." If we do not preserve the land and the animals on it there will be some kind of vengeance. But these are slow processes and people say, "Oh well, I can outlast it, why should I bother about posterity, what has posterity done for me?" So here we are. It is impossible to argue the case. Why should England's green and pleasant land remain green and pleasant? If I can have a comfortable little corner for myself that is good enough for me. Why should we bother about the magnificence and beauty of animals, if it only costs money? Why should we get together here and worry that with certain practices, wild life will be exterminated, will disappear? Why shouldn't it disappear? I can have a little bird in a cage if I need this kind of thing. You see, even threats do not work when it is a question of basic values and a question of the sacrifices that society is prepared to make for them.

All the same, it is not very difficult to demonstrate the magnitude of the long-term threat. I might point out that in the United Kingdom we are spending over one thousand four hundred million pounds a year on health—or rather on illness—a fantastic amount! Here we are supposed to have an affluent society, and having travelled very exhaustively in poor countries, I have never seen anywhere so much ill health as in the rich countries. In fact, health is no longer a real concept. The National Health Scheme is a great misnomer, it is the National Scheme to cope with sickness! With all the amazing improvement in medical knowledge and technique, the results are extraordinarily disappointing. The only thing that is easily measured is not health, but is length of life or life expectation. Since the year 1900, the life expectation of American males aged 45 has increased by 2.9 years, of males aged 65 by 1.2 years. Well, that is really nothing to write home about! In fact, a real advance has been made almost exclusively with infant mortality. That is a genuine advance in life saving. In the United States, the richest country in the world, according to recent findings over 41% of the entire population have chronic ailments, while the country is spending fifty thousand million dollars a year on health services. That is over £100 per person per year. With increasing affluence there is an increasing bill just to keep going and it is no longer a question of health, just a question of staying alive.

We can argue this and other points and can use them as threats, but it is impossible to make a real proof. People can always say, "You cannot impute ill-health to the use of land. Look at all the other factors!" Yes, we know, there are thousands of harmful habits, of unhealthy and frustrated ways of living. There is the cultivation of wholly unnecessary wants, totally contrary to all teaching that has ever been given to mankind. People quite proudly claim that what were luxuries for their fathers are necessities for them, which is just about the most devastating criticism that can be made of any way of life. There is the excessive urbanisation; there is the organisation of work in industry and commerce which for most people brings no real satisfaction. There is adulterated food;

there is aesthetic starvation. So who is going to prove how much of these tremendous bills for health can be imputed to any single factor such as the bad use of land?

It is no use trying to argue scientifically a point which is fundamentally a matter of faith. I know that this is not a popular thing to say, but there it is. For anyone who has the faith, there are the hallowed, wonderful statements to tell him precisely what it is all about. "And the Lord God took man and put him in the Garden of Eden," not to idle as a matter of fact, but "to dress it and keep it". And He also gave man "dominion over the fish in the sea and the fowl in the air, and over every living being that moves upon the earth." Mind you, dominion, not tyranny. The Lord God said "dress it and keep it"; He didn't say "ruin it and exterminate the animals". Those who do not have this faith, have some other faith and the matter becomes extremely involved. Normally, it is the faith in progress, which is quite impervious to threats in the long run, because it implies that the future will always and necessarily be better than the present. Any warning about the future tends to be dismissed as "one of those pessimisms so fashionable today". If the warning comes from an economist, he is not qualified to talk about the scientific side of things, if it comes from a scientist, he is not qualified to talk about an essentially economic problem, and so on. The faith in progress will not be challenged, and nobody is going to tell us that what we think is progress is in fact regress.

All the same, it is worthwhile noting what some thoughtful people are saying about these matters. I recommend the book by Lewis Herber on *Our Synthetic Environment* in which he says: "Metropolitan life is breaking down, psychologically, economically and biologically. Millions of people have acknowledged this breakdown by voting with their feet, they have picked up their belongings and left! If they have not been able to sever their connections with the metropolis at least they have tried. As a social symptom the effort is significant." He goes on to say, "Reconciliation of man with the natural world is no longer merely desirable, it has become a necessity."

I quote an American author because in many ways one can say that the Americans are twenty years ahead of us, and it is therefore always interesting to notice what is going on in the United States. Metropolitan life is breaking down psychologically, economically and biologically. Anyone who has been to the big American cities knows this to be true. But now, the remarkable fact is that it is equally true to say that, throughout the world rural life is breaking down, and we could use the same words that Herber used about metropolitan life. We could say that millions of people have acknowledged this breakdown by voting with their feet. They have picked up their belongings and left and gone to the big cities, where they have become slum dwellers. Town culture is breaking down because, of course, a town running into millions of inhabitants just does not make sense. A town with a sufficient concentration of people to generate a high culture makes sense, but not ten million inhabitants, and certainly not a town full of slums. In these vast towns the urban dweller is more isolated, says Mr. Herber, than his ancestors were in the countryside. "The city man in a modern metropolis has reached a degree of anonymity, social atomisation and spiritual isolation that is virtually unprecedented in human history." So what does he do? He tries to get into the suburbs and becomes a commuter. Well, isn't that what we are talking about— the multiple use of land? Here it is. He tries to get out, yet rural culture proper is breaking down and the rural people are trying to get in. This is the process that is going on all over the globe, in the rich countries as in the poor. And where the process has gone very far in the rich countries, you find no really healthy towns, but an immense sprawl of rich, bored, sterile suburbs, and also an immense city of terrible and degrading slums. This is equally true of India, poor India, as it is of rich America.

What are the remedies? This certainly is a very big situation that goes far beyond petty palliatives, and real remedies must begin at the basic question—what is worth bothering about? I listened to an exceedingly important European administrator the other day who said that "Nobody can afford the luxury of not acting economically". There was no chance of asking him whether he was acting economically when he chose to give his lecture. He looked clean-shaven to me, and I might have asked him if he was acting economically by shaving every day. But this is what he said, with great authority: "Nobody can afford the luxury of not acting economically." And this is all our problem hinges on: Are we prepared to face the fact that the luxury of not acting economically is precisely the right thing to do vis-à-vis air, water, other human beings and—the land?

Still, three questions of a practical kind arise. First of all, we should have to find agreement on what is proper land management, secondly, we should have to provide the legislation or the planning against abuses, and thirdly, we should have to see what could possibly be a sufficient incentive towards right behaviour. On any of these questions one would be foolish to speak dogmatically; we can only feel our way.

What would be proper land management? I do not want to go into the technicalities of it, about which I am not at all qualified to speak. But obviously the key ideas which must be brought back as respectable subjects of discussion are health, beauty and permanence. All three, I am sure, require an individual approach and individual care. When one thinks particularly of land in England, of the rolling hills where every field has its own characteristic, there is a world altogether different from the factory with standardised conditions. Everything requires individual care, a personal approach, the soil as well as the animals on the soil. But the trend is in exactly the opposite direction; it is towards depersonalisation and industrialisation. The trend is to centralise, to standardise, to concentrate. You ask a modern town dweller what he would consider proper land management, and he will say "maximum output and minimum cost"; that is his answer. There is no use beating about the bush, 90% of our people live in towns. They may not feel very proud about this answer, but that is the answer they give. Why should I have to pay for maintaining farming in Britain? It doesn't pay—let us import the food from other countries. Either the farmers should become economical or they should get out.

So this is the first question, to what extent can we increasingly achieve some agreement on what is proper land management. Is proper land management one of ever more concentration into an industrial type of farming, or is it in fact a personalised approach? Is it primarily orientated towards the idea of efficiency, or is it primarily orientated to the triple idea of health, beauty and permanence?

Second, what kind of legislation is one thinking of? Very important and very helpful steps have already been taken. There is zoning, there is planning—increasing work being done, about which we can all be fairly happy. There are important attempts to develop standards against extreme forms of factory farming. There are even some compulsory powers to dispossess in cases of very bad practice. All the same, it seems to me that what is really needed is a much more decentralised approach, a much more localised approach, and I think in the present state of affairs one cannot leave control entirely to officials. There should be something akin to the Committees we had during war time, where the users of land are judged by their peers.

Now, what about incentives, my third point? What about making it pay? If health, beauty and permanence are the primary goals, the key ideas, does it pay? Some of the land will be used for non-farming purposes, but for most of it the only use is farming. It is no use getting away from this fact by talking about the multiple use of land and saying that if farming does not pay the farmer can make a bit of money by taking in tourists. Either a tourist is overcharged and farming is subsidised out of that overcharge, or the farmer's wife is exploited and gets no proper reward for the services she renders to tourism, and farming is thereby subsidised by the farmer's wife. This, surely, is no answer to our problem. Of course there should be multiple use of land, and there always is multiple use of land because nothing can be done without some land; you cannot even build an apartment block or a factory. But the multiple use of land is not the answer to the problem of making farming pay.

Most of the land will either be derelict or, if we do not want that, it will have to be usefully employed in terms of farming. So we cannot get away from the fact that farming must pay, and the right kind of farming and the proper management of land must pay. It has been said "Why not pay the people who own the land a fee to keep it tidy and also to keep it available for us townies to spend a weekend?" Well, why not? We can, of course, decide that anyone who has so many acres and keeps them to a certain standard of tidiness and beauty, shall get a monetary reward. But in the end, let us not deceive ourselves, we are merely finding a slightly more involved justification for paying farming subsidies. And so the basic question remains, whether a mainly town-based civilisation is prepared to recognise the land as a value in itself. If subsidies are acceptable, as they are still today, I'm grateful to say, then I think they should be open subsidies, and they should be justified in these terms—as a common concern not only of the people working on the land, but of town and country people alike.

Everything is possible if society wants it. There are no technical difficulties, there is not a lack of knowledge. No economist needs to be consulted on "whether the country can afford" to look after its land. We know too much about ecology today to have any excuse for the many abuses that are now going on in the management of the land, in the management of animals, in food storage, food processing, food distribution, and in needless urbanisation. But as a society we have, at this point of time, no faith, no firm basis of belief in any meta-economic values, and when there is no such belief economics takes over. This is quite inevitable. How could it be otherwise? Nature, it has been said, abhors a vacuum, and when the available space is not filled by some higher motivation, then it will be filled by something lower, by the small, mean, calculating attitude to life which is rationalised in the economic calculus.

I have no doubt that a callous attitude to the land and to the animals thereon is connected with, and symptomatic of, a great many other attitudes, such as those producing heedless urbanisation, needless industrialisation, and a kind of fanaticism which insists on playing about with novelties—technical, chemical, biological and so forth—long before their long-term consequences are even remotely understood. In the simple question of how we treat the land, I am sure, our entire way of life is involved, and before our policies with regard to the land will really be changed, there will have to be a great deal of philosophical, not to say religious, change.

That is why I do not wish to suggest that all that is needed is a clever economist to produce some brilliant formula on how to get a proper treatment of land without anyone noticing the cost. Noticeable costs there will be, and it needs nothing less than a general return to a recognition of meta-economic values for society to be prepared to bear them.

Vol 2 No 7, May-June 1969

Chapter 17

How to Abolish Land Speculation

NO ONE CAN EXIST without some land base. With growing population, growing mobility, growing production, growing trade, land values tend to move up and up on a one-way street (quite apart from inflation). Anyone who manages to 'corner' land only has to wait to grow rich. Karl Marx, Henry George, and countless others have pointed to the absurdity and injustice of land speculation; but the free enterprise system has never done anything effective to stop it.

Calls for land nationalisation have gone unanswered because few people could see it as a valid alternative to private ownership. To start with, how could the State ever find the money to buy out the existing owners? And even if the money could be found, there is reason to fear that State ownership of land would automatically and inevitably mean some type of bureaucratic administration—a daunting prospect indeed.

In order to abolish land speculation, it is not necessary to abolish decentralised ownership. The direct relationship between a person and a piece of land is something so elementary and satisfying that one would hesitate a long time before abolishing it. To adopt State ownership of land just for the purpose of abolishing land speculation would be like jumping from the frying pan into the fire.

All that needs doing to stop land speculation is to establish the rule that no landowner may ever receive for any piece of land more than its 'registered value'.

Every piece of land in the United Kingdom has a certain value or price as of now—say, as of September 1st, 1974. If the owner sold it now, he or she would have some idea of what it would fetch, perhaps after taking professional advice. If he/she died, the value of the land would be assessed as part of his/her estate. Let us say the value of every piece of land in the United Kingdom were to be ascertained: this would no doubt be a big job but by no means an impossible one. Values would reflect the current zoning arrangements (as of September 1st, 1974) and many other price-determining factors. The ascertained value would be registered with the Local Authority and be called the 'registered value'. To take care of future inflation, the Government would publish an index showing what the pound sterling was worth compared with its worth on September 1st, 1974, and whenever a transaction were to take place, the 'registered value' would be adjusted according to the index. So the 'registered value', adjusted for inflation, would always remain the same in real terms. Anyone who wanted to sell land at any future date would know that he or she could never obtain more for it than this inflation-adjusted 'registered value'. This would be the basic principle—very simple and, I suggest, unquestionably just—if land speculation is to be abolished.

But what would happen if someone wished to sell land which, through re-zoning or some other change, had become much more valuable? Whenever land comes up for sale which has risen in value owing to the operation of social forces (such as re-zoning or 'planning permission') the Local Authority should have the right of first refusal, that is to say, to buy such land at a competitive price, the sort of price a private purchaser would be willing to pay for it. If it made use of its right to purchase, it would pay the seller the 'registered value' and pay any surplus into a special fund which might be called the Local Authority Land Fund. If it did not choose to make use of its right to purchase, a private purchaser would have the opportunity of buying the land in question, and he/she would do exactly the same—pay the seller the 'registered value' and remit the surplus to the Local Authority Land Fund.

And what would become of the 'registered value' then? If a higher price had in fact been paid in the manner described, whether by a Local Authority or by any other purchaser, this would then become the new 'registered value'. In other words, the 'registered value' would never be less than what (after the date of the initial assessment—September 1st, 1974) a new purchaser had actually paid for his land.

It may of course happen that a piece of land is for sale and no one is willing to pay for it as much as the 'registered value'. A transaction between willing seller and willing buyer may then take place at a lower price, which then becomes the 'registered value'.

In short, the current owner and any subsequent buyer are deprived of the chance of making any windfall profits through land ownership; all such profits go automatically into the public hand, the Local Authority Land Fund. In those exceptional cases where a particular piece of land declines in value, the seller may indeed fail to recover the 'registered value', but that is the risk he takes in buying land or, if you like, the price he pays for the immense privilege of private land ownership.

Needless to say, any scheme, even one of the greatest simplicity, like the one here proposed, raises some complicated questions. What about buildings and other structures on the land? What if I have acquired a piece of land and have built a road or a house or some other building that has cost me a great deal of money? Can I recover my expenditure on 'improvements' when I want to sell my land? These 'improvements' will not be reflected by the 'registered value' of the land.

This is not an insuperable difficulty. Although there does not exist—and cannot be—a precise science of valuation, it is possible to come to reasonable solutions of the problem. Valuers can distinguish between 'site (or land) value' and the value of buildings and other structures.

Another objection to these proposals is this: If people have land they do not need and cannot make vast profits on selling it, they will simply keep it, refusing to sell; and so, a great amount of land which society needs will be hoarded and withheld from proper use. This is not a valid objection. Powers of compulsory purchase exist, and although they should never be used except as a power of last resort, their existence is accepted by society and they suffice to deal with anti-social behaviour.

I commend this scheme for further thought. I claim that it would produce a genuine middle-way solution to the problem of land ownership and a total solution to the problem of land speculation. The new dispensation would become active only as and when the landowner wishes to get rid of his land—in other words, when he wishes to cease being a landowner. Most landowners in any case are farmers, and nothing could be further from their real interests and predilections than land speculation.

The elimination of land speculation would greatly increase the ability of local authorities to obtain land for public needs at fair prices, and this proposal would siphon into the public hand all windfall gains from the growing scarcity of land. I hardly think there is need to explain what the monies accumulating in the Local Authority Land Fund might be earmarked for. Private affluence and public squalor is one of the besetting sins of the modern world. Yet, if monies are channelled into public hands, the problem of how to achieve democratic control over their expenditure still remains. I am not claiming that a scheme to eliminate land speculation will solve this problem. But if we do set our minds on eliminating land speculation, critics of this proposal may fairly be asked: "Alright, if you don't like this scheme, will you kindly propose something better?"

Vol 5 No 4, Sept-Oct 1974

SPIRITUALITY
& NON-VIOLENCE

The Roots of Violence

NON-VIOLENCE, IT SEEMS, is only for saints; and while it is assuredly the task of all men and women to strive for sainthood, there are but few of us who get near enough to this goal to be able to be firm in nonviolence—when it comes to the test. It seems, therefore, that we must learn to live with Violence. We may have a chance to curb it, but hardly a chance to make it wither away altogether.

The itch of violence is a part of human nature. It might be said that it is the task of civilisation to control, channel, or sublimate it. Modern civilisation appears, indeed, to channel violence away from everyday inter-human relations, but then, instead of sublimating it seems to multiply it a million-fold. The Bomb is the symbol of modern civilisation. Unfortunately, it is not merely a symbol but an ever-present threat to all life on our planet, yet it is also a symbol of a civilisation that has bred readiness for violence without any limit whatsoever. The reader may object to the use of the word 'readiness'. But if we, or our masters, were not ready to use The Bomb in certain circumstances, we should not go to the painful expense of having it at all. Only if we were willing to say: "We shall not use The Bomb in any circumstances whatsoever", could we claim not to be ready to use it. But in that case, of course, we should have no Bomb.

Far from curbing our readiness to engage in violence on the ultimate scale, it would appear, therefore, that modern civilisation has actually produced it. How could this be possible? How is it possible for the same civilisation simultaneously and concurrently to produce a great curbing of violence at the level of inter-human relations and the ultimate perfection of violence at the level of international relations?

The answer normally given to this question suggests that our relative nonviolence at the personal level is simply due to the existence of the police and the Rule of Law, the only way to achieve the same at the international level would be to set up an international police force and introduce an international Rule of Law. There is, of course, some truth in this answer, but I do not think it goes to the root of the matter.

Let us try to find the roots of violence. Some people, of course, consider it sufficient to point to original sin. If there were not something profoundly unsatisfactory about human nature, history would not he such a record of crime, culminating in the threat of total extermination as a 'deterrent'. This unsatisfactoriness is no doubt a compound of moral weakness, normally called sin, and intellectual weakness, normally called ignorance. To put all the blame on Sin betrays considerable intellectual weakness, and to put all the blame on Ignorance betrays a lack of candour which can only be due to considerable moral weakness. However that may be, all this is rather too general for our purpose.

As we are a compound of mind and body, we may not go far wrong by looking for the roots of violence both in the body and in the mind. In fact, this is exactly what traditional moral philosophy has always done. In the West, we had the teaching of the Seven Deadly Sins, which were made up of three 'warm' sins and three 'cold' ones, while the seventh, *acedia* or Sloth, is neither warm nor cold. As Dorothy Sayers put it, "in the world it calls itself Tolerance; but in hell it is called Despair. . . It is the sin which believes in nothing, cares for nothing, seeks to know nothing, interferes with nothing, enjoys nothing, loves nothing, hates nothing, finds purpose in nothing, lives for nothing, and only remains alive because there is nothing it would die for". No deep roots of violence here.

Among the three 'warm' sins—*luxuria* which we call Lust; *gula* which we call Gluttony; and ire which we call Wrath—there are undoubtedly deep roots of violence to be found in ire. The 'warm' sins arise primarily from the body, from the 'heart' if you like, and there violence tends to be counterbalanced or checked by strong emotional forces like pity, mercy, and a liability to get tired and disgusted. In the present phase of modern civilisation, these warm-hearted sins are not a great threat, nor are they taken seriously, but merely considered somewhat vulgar.

It is different with the 'cold' sins. They are not generally thought of as sins at all, but as admirable or at least perfectly normal traits of character. The three 'cold' sins, arising from the mind, are called *avaritia* or Covetousness; *invidia* or Envy; and *superbia* or Pride. The roots of violence grow in all three, and there is little, if anything, in the natural dispositions of the mind to counteract or check their force.

The old teaching of the Deadly Sins recognises that the violence that stems from the heart tends quickly to find its limits: it is checked by other powerful emotions; while the violence that stems from the mind is capable of becoming unlimited and transgressing all bounds. From this it may be deduced that a civilisation which glorifies the mind at the expense of the heart is in constant danger of slipping into limitless violence; while a civilisation which glorified the heart at the expense of the mind would be in danger of sporadic brutalities without rhyme or reason.

There can be no doubt that our civilisation claims as its greatest achievement the 'objectivity' of its thought, which has led, for all to see, to the most astonishing achievements of science and technology. This capability of the mind, called 'objectivity', depends on the rejection and suppression of all emotional forces other than the desire to solve the problem at hand. This is sometimes called a desire for truth or the "irresistible need to explore" (Bronowski), but whatever it may be called, it is cold, detached heartless, efficient, and relentless. Pure objectivity is possible only when Reason operates outside the control of the heart. It can then ask any questions without a shudder; it can treat any matter of investigation as an object alone, not as anything that feels, that has a sense of feeling of itself. Working through the mind alone, you can study a blind man 'objectively' and describe him as if he were a mechanical puppet—which is also blind; working through the heart you might shut your own eyes in an attempt to get the feeling of blindness yourself, subjectively.

The violence that stems from the mind, from the three 'cold' sins, has the power of objectivity, untrammelled by any subjective participation with the experience of the violated. It is like signing a death warrant or launching an inter-continental missile: the more 'objectively' it is done, the easier it is. It comes out of pure thought.

Thought is much lighter, freer and swifter than action. We are capable of thinking actions which we would never perform. The logical sequence from thought to speech to action is a sequence of increasing incarnation or substantialisation, a movement from mind to body, or from 'cold' to 'warm', from invisible to visible, or, we can also say, from objectivity to subjectivity. With the individual person, there is always the chance, and even the likelihood, that the heart or body, that is to say his subjectivity, will control and inhibit the extravagances of his mind, his thought, his objectivity. But when there is organisation and specialisation, this chain is broken: No. 1 has the idea; No. 2 gives the order, and No. 3 carries it out. If No. 3's action is one of detestable violence, who is to blame? Who is responsible? Of course, all three are responsible but in descending order.

Yet, modem civilisation, pragmatic, positivist, and objective, can see and appreciate only the visible, and guilt seems to be distributed in ascending order. No. 3, the person of action, is the guilty one—the others have only thought and talked.

We therefore like to think of Eichmann as a monster, and then discover him to be very ordinary indeed, a meek little man, trained in objectivity; a man who has no 'warm' vices that move him to violence; a man who couldn't hurt a fly. His actions were not controlled by the heart, but by some very simple rules of the mind—rules of objectivity untrammelled by emotion, like a computer programmed in a certain way.

The Eichmann phenomenon demonstrates that detached, objective thought, always liable to error, opens the door to unlimited violence because it eliminates the countervailing power of the heart. A civilisation which deprecates the heart, which idolises objectivity in the forms of scientism, positivism, and rationalism, which bases its entire education on the notion that decisions must he taken without interference from the emotions, inevitably exposes itself to the dangers of unlimited violence.

This trait of modern civilisation can be traced through all fields of human activity. Take economics and the pursuit of 'higher living standards'. All promptings of the heart are dismissed as sentimentality and lack of realism: to think of people rather than of profit is 'uneconomic'. To take the future as seriously as we are naturally inclined to take the present is being discouraged by the theory of 'discounted cash flow' which systematically devalues the future. Hence the unlimited exploitation and despoliation of Nature—a perverse implementation of the words "take no thought of tomorrow".

When the violence of economic strivings comes from the 'warm' sins of Lust, Gluttony, or Wrath, that is to say, mainly from the body—or the heart—it carries within itself a self-limiting principle and is capable of saying Enough. But when it comes from the 'cold' sins of Covetousness, Envy, and Pride, that is to say, mainly from the mind, trained in objectivity, there is no self-limiting principle, no idea of Enough: the sky is the limit. The higher the level of wealth already attained, the greater is the fanaticism for further 'growth'.

Conquest of Nature and of Space; the 'irresistible need to explore'; unlimited economic expansion; etc.—these are the concepts of violence. The concepts of non-violence would be Reverence for Life; religious 'Praise'; humility; measure, in the sense of knowing where to stop; and an irresistible need for justice. The former derive from minds unchecked by the heart; the latter derive from hearts that are strong enough to control the mind.

The violence that is in the process of destroying the world is the cold, calculating, detached, heartless, and relentless violence that springs from over-extended minds working out of control of under-developed hearts. A person who does not feel his thoughts but merely entertains them, who has trained the objectivity of his mind at the expense of the subjectivity of his heart, is capable of limitless violence while never losing his temper, never falling into the 'warm' sins of Lust, Gluttony, or Wrath. He shakes his head in sorrow or contempt over the vulgarity and irrationality of people who are still so underdeveloped that they fall into warm-hearted sins. He is supremely rational; for him, the only certainty is his own death, and, objectively seen, his own death is equivalent to the disappearance of the world. He stands at the pinnacle of egocentricity and potential violence. Pure reason can worship only itself, and only the heart can conceive the idea of sacrifice.

Modern civilisation can survive only if it begins again to educate the heart, which is the source of Wisdom; for modern human beings are now far too clever to be able to survive without wisdom.

Vol 7 No 6, Jan-Feb 1977

Asia Undermined

THE DILEMMA I AM GOING TO WRITE ABOUT is due to the impact of the modern West upon the ancient East. This impact necessarily produces a crisis of the greatest possible magnitude, because the modern West challenges and tends to destroy everything that Asia has held sacred, everything from which Asian thought and life have been nourished for thousands of years—everything, in fact, which is Asia's own.

The antithesis, however, is not between West and East, between Occident and Orient, but between the modern way of life, a unique 'deviation' in history, which at present prevails in the West, and the traditional or normal way of life which still survives, however precariously, in the East. Our own forefathers before the Renaissance, if suddenly resurrected today, would unquestionably feel more at home in what remains of the ancient East than in Western Europe or America.

The dilemma of Asia is a spiritual dilemma, because all her spiritual values and attainments are at stake. In saying this I am attributing 'reality' to spiritual matters.

The fundamental question, asked by all peoples at all times, is "What is man?" And the answer given by the universal tradition of mankind is that man is a compound of spirit, soul, and body. (Some people would say "soul, mind, and body", but I prefer the words I have used.) Occasionally, people lose the ability of distinguishing between spirit and soul, and then man is described simply as a compound of body and soul. Then they are in imminent danger of losing even the soul, for body and soul are so closely connected that it is not difficult to make out a case that they are merely two aspects of one and the same thing.

In all civilisations we can observe occasional tendencies to this kind of simplification, but normally they are quickly overcome and forgotten. The modern West is the only significant exception. All other civilisations are—or at any rate used to be—primarily interested in spiritual matters; they saw the spirit as the divine and, generally, immortal element, equipped with a psychosomatic instrument, the embodied soul or, if you like, the ensouled body.

Naturally, if there is such an element which is divine and immortal, it deserves infinitely more attention than its instrument, the soul-body, which is so dependent, so changeable, and so obviously mortal. Hence the whole of life revolved around the spirit as the only 'reality', body and soul and everything pertaining to them being considered relatively unreal.

In Europe, we have moved away from all this during the last three centuries or so. The modern West is not preoccupied with spiritual matters, but with material matters instead. Yet a certain awareness remains even with us; the term' 'spiritual' still exists in our language, although a highly esteemed school of philosophers tells us that it has no meaning.

The moment one takes the idea of the 'spirit' seriously one is driven to conclusions which are in no way fashionable today. If one believes that matters of the spirit are 'real' and therewith infinitely important, and that matters pertaining to body and soul are only relatively real (which means somewhat unreal) and gain their importance only from the fact that the body-soul is an instrument of the spirit—just as a workman's tools derive their importance solely from the person who uses them; if one believes that, one can recognise that Asia is involved not merely in political and economic difficulties but in a genuine 'spiritual crisis'.

Those who do not believe in any of this, those who take man as nothing but an intelligent animal accidentally thrown up by the process of evolution, etc. etc., will not, I am afraid, get anything in this article with which they could possibly agree. Since, as far as they are concerned, there is no spirit, there can be no spiritual dilemma of Asia or of anybody else.

Why speak of a 'spiritual dilemma', they say. Is there not simply a battle between modern knowledge and ancient error, between progress and reaction, between the advanced and the backward? This is what we are told from morning to night, often with the best intentions. The modern West must help the backward East; the rich must help the poor. Of course, we must respect them; we must not feel superior because that would arouse antagonism; but as a matter of fact we are superior as we have the answers and they haven't.

Admittedly, we are no longer quite as prone as we used to be to put these ideas into words (as I have just done), but our new humility, it seems to me, is a mock humility, because in fact we are maintaining the notion that nothing really counts except our own latest attainments. Western people, in short, still believe in their 'civilising mission', and they are supported in this by the great majority of westernised orientals whose belief in Western superiority is even more uncritical than our own.

Against these 'progressive' opinions, I hold the view that there is a spiritual dilemma and that what is being destroyed in Asia is not merely error, reaction, and backwardness, but an altogether priceless heritage for which we—and they—are substituting nothing but triviality and disorder.

It is impossible to obtain even the most superficial appreciation of this heritage unless we purge our minds completely of two or three deep-rooted prejudices. The first one, already alluded to, is the white people's implicit belief in the superiority of the white race over all other races. This superiority in fact exists in the purely material realm—a recent phenomenon already in decline—but is more than out-balanced today by a marked inferiority in some other respects. The second prejudice is the implicit belief in the superiority of contemporary white people over all previous generations of the white race. This belief is so deep-rooted that it survives all rational argument to the contrary. It is inculcated into our children from the moment they begin to learn: "Of course, in the olden days they did not know" or "Think of it, this was already known so many hundreds of years ago", etc. etc. Both these prejudices are supported and deepened by a complementary contraction in our experience of reality: only the material realm constitutes reality for modern westerners, and since in this particular field they are indeed superior both to their ancestors and to their coloured contemporaries, their very deficiency supports their superiority complex.

While the great majority of Westerners have lost all contact with spiritual reality, many of them none the less still adhere to a certain pseudo-Christianity and this becomes an opportunity for them to indulge in a third prejudice of the most pernicious kind: Christianity is the only true religion; all non-Christians are heathens steeped in idol worship. As Ananda Coomaraswamy said

(*The Bugbear of Literacy*, p.49): "The one outstanding, and perhaps the only, real heresy of modern Christianity in the eyes of other believers is its claim to exclusive truth; for this is treason against Him who 'never left himself without a witness' and can only be paralleled by Peter's denial of Christ; and whoever says to his pagan friends that 'the light that is in you is darkness', in offending these is offending the Father of lights." Even Christian tolerance of the other religions is often not more than mockery. "There can be no more vicious kind of tolerance than to approach another man to tell him that 'We are both serving the same God, you in your way and I in His.' ' (p.48)

You can see that these three prejudices between them cover the ground pretty well. To those of us who recognise only the material realm as real, everything confirms the superiority of the modern West. And those to whom religion is a real and important thing in the world can base their feeling of superiority on the staggering claim that their own Christian religion is not merely true but the only true religion in the world. What, then, could Asia offer that is worthy of preservation either for the Asians themselves or for the world as a whole? The three prejudices suggest only one answer: Nothing at all. By all means, preserve a bit of the mystery and the glamour; this will come in useful as a tourist attraction; but away with the rest!

This is more or less the official attitude. "We are talking about transforming whole societies", said Mr. Eugene Black, the former President of the World Bank, when lecturing on 'The Age of Economic Development', "and creating new traditions to replace traditions which have been rendered tragically inadequate by the passing of time." And what are these so-called "new traditions"? (The expression reminds one of the story of some American university administration announcing that all students will henceforth dress in such and such a way: "This tradition will start at 10 a.m. tomorrow.") They imply the unreserved acceptance of what may be called the religion of economics. Of course Mr Eugene Black does not call it that. He says that "there is real hope that people will take ideology less seriously simply because they will be too busy". It is hoped that they will imitate the modern West because, according to Mr Black, "it is largely. . . by not taking ideology too seriously that the western world to-day enjoys democracy and freedom as well as the highest material living standards." In short, it is necessary to care for nothing but economics, and Mr Black will make it easy: he will "render the language of economics. . . morally antiseptic". People must not feel that caring for economics alone, is also an ideology; therefore—"We try to remove the taint of ideology from the language of economics and thus relate that language solely to the end of promoting higher material living standards."

The attempt to transform whole societies certainly does not suffer from an excess of modesty. It rests on a superiority complex so deep-rooted and so free from doubt that even the severest adverse experiences in practical life cannot shake it. "Economic development," says Mr Black, referring to the underdeveloped countries, "has proved peculiarly fickle; even now it is creating human desires much faster than it is providing means for their gratification." Is it therefore necessary to reconsider the whole approach? Oh no, continues Mr Black. "Economic development has left in its wake in the underdeveloped world tragic problems *which only more economic development can solve*." [Italics added]

It would be quite unfair to consider these opinions as peculiar to Mr Black, a leading banker. They are fully representative of the dominant thought in the modern West and accurately depict the image created by Western aid in the so-called under-developed countries.

Here is an ideology of the greatest possible aggressiveness, offering the greatest possible temptations. It has been approvingly described by Professor Donald J. Dewey, of Duke University, as follows: "The concern for efficiency and progress is—and always has been—secular in that it condemns all religious restraints that are inimical to higher man-hour productivity. This concern is unromantic in that it will not sacrifice national income in order to maintain a happy peasantry or a culture-carrying leisure class. It is materialistic in that happiness is regarded as a more pressing goal—if not a more worthy goal—than salvation. And above all, it is optimistic in that it supposes that the sum of human happiness is increased by growing wealth."

It would be hard to deny that this absurdly barbarous statement reflects a condition of extraordinary unbalance, justifying René Guenon's harsh words that "Western civilisation is an anomaly, not to say a monstrosity". No wonder that the illustrious late president of India, Radhakrishnan, has come to the conclusions that "civilisation is not worth saving if it continues on its present foundations". Yet it represents the height of temptation, tending to corrupt, if it were possible, even the elect.

For the last hundred years there has been a growing conviction among the spiritual élite of Asia that the onslaught of temptation coming from the modern West would prove irresistible, and that it might become impossible to preserve the treasures of traditional culture accumulated over the ages. The most sacred texts, previously accessible only to the initiated, have therefore been released to Western scholars who have invested an immense amount of labour to edit, translate and interpret them. During the nineteenth century, most of these translations and interpretations were so much coloured and distorted by the spirit of crude materialism which was then reigning supreme in Europe that they altogether failed to convey the subtlety and sublimity of the Eastern teachings. But since then, there has been a small group of devoted people from many Western countries who not merely learned the words but also entered into the spirit of the teachings.

And what do we find? We find that this culture is the outcome of a sustained struggle, carried on over many thousands of years, to uphold and develop what is good in human beings and to weaken and control what is evil; to promote in every way the Good, the True and the Beautiful, as Plato would say; but, above all to obtain salvation by the way of Knowledge. This is not a knowledge of facts, which is merely useful, but a "knowledge that can make you free". It results not simply from an operation of the reasoning power, but from an engagement of the whole person, body, soul and spirit. It is knowledge which Europe used to possess—no people has ever been left without it—but which we have increasingly rejected and now lost. Let me quote Ananda Coomaraswamy: "If we leave out of account the 'modernistic' and individual philosophies of today, and consider only the great tradition of the magnanimous philosophers, whose philosophy was a religion that had to be lived if it was to be understood, it will soon be found that the distinctions of culture in East and West, or for that matter North and South, are comparable only to those of dialects; all are speaking what is essentially one and the same spiritual language, employing different words, but expressing the same ideas, and very often by means of identical idioms. Otherwise stated, there is a universally intelligible language, not only verbal but also visual, of the fundamental ideas on which the different civilisations have been founded." (*Bugbear*, p.78).

This universally intelligible language is still alive in Asia today. In spite of the tremendous noise made by westernised functionaries, it can still be heard by those who have shed their prejudices and are willing to learn. Modernisation and industrialisation still have not proceeded so far as to eliminate the traditional way of life altogether, so that it is yet possible to see in actual life what a "balanced" civilisation really means.

The bases of modern civilisation, it has been said, are such "that it has been forgotten even by the learned that man ever attempted to live otherwise than by bread alone." (Coomaraswamy, p.7) In Asia, however, this attempt can still be seen in action in a few places not yet spoiled by the "withering touch" of Westernisation. There is still "right livelihood", pride of craftsmanship, beauty, and dignity—even where by Western standards people live in poverty. There is still a way of life where every man and woman can be an artist and through his or her creativeness obtain true knowledge, and where all genuine knowledge is held in veneration. The late Sir George Birdwood, himself a convinced and exemplary Christian, upon encountering such a society in India said that "such an ideal order we should have held impossible of realisation, but it continues to exist. . . and to afford us, in the yet living results of its daily operation in India, a proof of the superiority, in so many unsuspected ways, of the hieratic civilisation of antiquity over the secular, joyless, inane, and self-destructive civilisation of the West". (quoted pp.80-81)

The modern mind is incapable of understanding that a genuine attachment to and knowledge of spiritual matters is capable of producing something like an 'ideal order' in the external life—that in fact it is the inescapable pre-condition for such an order. "Seek ye first the kingdom of God and all these things shall be added on to you"—how well these words are known and how utterly repudiated by the modern West, which calls itself Christian. The truth is that we can see these two approaches only as irreconcilable opposites: either you seek the kingdom of God and His righteousness or you seek "all these things" , namely order, welfare, well-being and happiness. As the American professor said: "Happiness is regarded as a more pressing goal—if not a more worthy goal—than salvation," and we condemn "all religious restraints that are inimical to higher man-hour productivity". But when we turn to Asia we find a living tradition of knowledge and wisdom, which includes practice in daily life, based upon 'restraint', upon the control and overcoming of 'desire', upon 'liberation'. It would be quite wrong to suggest that the 'ideal order' still exists which Sir George Birdwood found some seventy years ago; but traces of it still exist together with the perennial wisdom. As we would say today, the 'know-how' still exists, not merely in words and theories but as a living force in millions of people.

Now, I think, we can see the spiritual dilemma: the old order has broken down and this breakdown has brought appalling poverty; now there beckons a new order, developed by the modern West, which suggests that the poverty can be overcome only by making a still more radical break with all old traditions; it suggests not that Asiatic poverty is due to the breakdown of an almost ideal order, but on the contrary that it is due to the survival of some elements of that order.

The stark facts of poverty in Asia shall of course not be denied or belittled in any way. But it is a grave error to imagine that there had never been anything but dire misery for the great mass of humanity in traditional societies. This is a part of the modernistic prejudice which completely falsifies history. The present poverty is in no way typical of conditions during the many thousands of years of Asian history. On the contrary, it is most exceptional and is in fact mainly the result of that 'withering touch' of the West which came not only with overwhelming physical power but also with the glitter of an almost irresistible temptation. It is the result of a long drawn-out process of decay which started at the spiritual level and is now manifesting on the physical level for all to see.

Few people deny that 'something needs to be done'. But what? Mr Eugene Black, whom I have already quoted, says, in effect, that Westernisation has created tragic problems which can be solved only by more Westernisation. Others also say that Westernisation has created tragic problems, but conclude that what is needed is a return to the true principles of their own, indigenous civilisation.

This is not a conflict of opinion between one group wanting material improvements and another group rejecting them in favour of so-called spiritual values. No, *both* groups want material improvements. There is no authentic spiritual teaching that enjoins people to neglect their material conditions and to vegetate in misery. It is not a denial of spiritual values for starving people to search for bread instead of attending to religious functions. While both groups, as I said, want material improvements, the one group believes them to be attainable only by following the Western way, which is anti-traditional and anti-spiritual, and the other group believes that material improvements can come only from a modern revival of the traditional way of life. Or to put it negatively, the one group (which is by far the most vociferous) says: "You cannot have economic development unless you are prepared to abandon your spiritual traditions and preoccupations and adopt the 'religion of economics'", while the other group says: "You cannot have economic development unless you are prepared to strengthen and purify your spiritual traditions and preoccupations."

You will not be surprised if I say that the type or pattern of economic development which these two contending groups have in mind is not the same. The one is modern and Western; the other is derived from indigenous traditions of great antiquity. The one puts the accent on quantity; the other, on quality. The one is mainly concerned with the satisfactions derivable from consumption; the other, with the dignity and creativity of people as producers. The one degrades labour and then tries to save it; the other ennobles labour and uses it freely. The crucial question in both cases is how the process of development is to get started. The trump card in the hands of the Westernisers is that they can make a plan and—perhaps—carry it through, if necessary by force. But their chief weakness is that a plan which has no roots among the people may altogether fail to win popular support and to yield results of real benefit to the people.

Herein, it seems to me, lies the present predicament of India. Even where the plans are being fulfilled, there is no real success. The other group, with more respect for the indigenous wisdom, insists that only self-help can be ultimately effective and can multiply a million-fold by spreading all over the country. They are instinctively against central planning, which always tends to assume a

Western bias, and wish to rely on spontaneous growth coming
from the people themselves, from the villages, unorganised, free,
unplanned, unpredictable. But what if it does not come sponta-
neously? You may wait in vain for the people to bestir themselves,
and even a great living saint, like Vinoba Bhave in India, may not
be able to inspire and arouse them sufficiently for constructive
action, at least, not as quickly as you may wish.

This is the eternal question, and I am not pretending that I
could answer it. If there were a definitive answer, we would long
ago have solved all our problems. Nothing is ever accomplished
except by creative individuals; but individuals alone can do nothing. How can they get the support and co-operation of the passive
majority? Nothing of value can be accomplished except on the
basis of spontaneity and freedom; but the passive majority, being
passive, is lacking precisely in spontaneity and tends to move only
under duress.

There are, as far as I can see, only two forces which can
resolve these paradoxical problems—great suffering or great wisdom. In China, there has been very great suffering ever since the
collapse of the Manchu Empire, and the suffering has produced
both the 'cadres' of men and women of steel to lead the masses
and the readiness of the masses to be led. In India, there exists
great wisdom—can it be made fruitful? The tragedy is that many
educated Indians imagine that the suffering can be avoided by
giving up the wisdom.

A few words about the value of that wisdom for the West. I cannot do better than quote from Marco Pallis's foreword to one of
René Guenon's books:

> The present situation of the West is. . . to be compared to that
> of the foolish virgins who, through the wandering of their
> attention in other directions, had allowed their lamps to go out;
> in order to rekindle the sacred fire, which in its essence is always
> the same wherever it may be burning, they must have recourse
> to the lamps still kept alight by their wiser companions; but
> once relighted, it will still be their own lamps that they will be
> lighted by, and all they will then have to do is to keep them
> properly fed with the kind of oil at their own disposal. . . A
> Hindu somewhere has written that the inability of Westerners

to interpret the East is bound up with their failure to penetrate the deeper meaning of their own sages and even of the Gospels. Reciprocally, it may be said that by a genuine assimilation of the essential content of the Eastern traditions, they might be helped to recapture the spirit that dwells at the heart of Christianity itself. . .

If for the Westerner a true knowledge of the traditional doctrines offers the only effective means of escaping the impending disaster that so many dread but feel powerless to prevent, through a process of inward reintegration and of reform in the literal sense of the word, so also for the Easterner it remains the indispensable means of consolidation, self-renewal, independence and recollection.

"All civilisations have decayed; only they have decayed in different ways; the decay of the East is passive and that of the West is active." (Schuon, *Perspectives*, p. 22) "The East is sleeping over truths; the West lives in errors." Who is it that most requires aid? Unquestionably the West, because it is being helplessly driven on by demonic forces which may at any time destroy the world. In the names of individualism, freedom, and democracy it has abandoned the struggle against the evil propensities of human nature and is utterly unprincipled even where it is attempting to do good.

To get into real contact with the wisdom of India and China constitutes not only a priceless personal gain but also a unique chance to discover what we have to do politically and economically to avoid utter ruin. Neither for Asia nor for the West is there a spiritual dilemma. But there is temptation. For both there is the choice between serving God or Mammon. It is a part of the modern error to believe that this is equivalent to a choice between poverty and riches. It is not. On the contrary, all appearances notwithstanding, the service of Mammon is not reward by lasting prosperity, but by cataclysmic disaster. It is the service of God—or of Truth, as Asia would say—that alone leads to lasting well-being on this earth.

Vol 7 No 3, July-Aug 1976

Chapter 20

Message from the Universe

OUR 'ENVIRONMENT', IT MIGHT BE SAID, is the Universe *minus* ourselves. If it is felt today that all is not well with the environment—so that it even requires the protection of its own Secretary of State—the complaint is not about the Universe as such but about our impact upon it. This impact is seen to produce, all too often, two deleterious effects: the destruction of natural beauty, which is bad enough, and the destruction of what is called 'ecological balance' or the health and life-sustaining power of the biosphere, which is even worse. I shall refer mainly to the second one of these concerns, that is to say, to what we are doing to the living world around us.

Who is 'we' in this connection? Is it people-in-general? Is it world population? Is it anybody and everybody'? No, it is not anybody and everybody. The great majority of people, even today, are living in a manner which does not seriously damage the biosphere or deplete the world's resource endowment. These are the people living in traditional cultures. We generally refer to them as the world's poor, *because we are more aware of their poverty than of their culture.* Many of them are getting poorer in the sense that they are losing their most precious possession, i.e. their own traditional culture, which is rapidly breaking down. In some cases one is entitled to say that they are getting much poorer while getting a little bit richer. As they abandon their traditional life-styles and adopt that of the modern West, they may also have an increasingly damaging impact upon the environment.

The fact remains, all the same, that it is not the great numbers of the world's poor that are endangering Spaceship Earth but the relatively small numbers of the world's rich. The threat to the environment, and in particular to world resources and the biosphere, comes from the life-style of the rich societies and not from that of the poor. Even in the poor societies there are some rich people, and as long as they adhere to their traditional culture they do very little,

if any, harm. ɪt is only when they become 'westernised' that damage to the environment ensues. This shows that our problem is
somewhat complicated. It is not simply a matter of rich or poor—
rich being harmful and poor being harmless. It is a matter of
life-styles. A poor American may do much more ecological damage
than a rich Asian.

To grasp the meaning of 'life-style' is not at all easy. Our most
fundamental attitudes and convictions are involved, in other
words, our metaphysics or our religion. To put the matter at its
simplest: it is a question of what we consider to be our needs. It
is clear that we have many needs, some physical and some spiritual. Our physical needs, like all physical things, are obviously
limited. But our spiritual needs are in a sense unlimited: they transcend 'this world'. If it is said that 'man doth not live by bread
alone, but by every word that proceedeth out of the mouth of the
Lord', this is not simply a bit of moralising but a statement of fact.
(See Deut. 8:3)

A civilisation which devotes its attention primarily and almost
exclusively to material advancement—I say *almost* exclusively,
because the total exclusion of other concerns would make survival
impossible—such a civilisation, as it progresses in science and technology, will tend to develop a life-style which makes ever increasing demands upon the physical environment. Take the need to get
beyond, to transcend, 'this world'. People who understand that
'man doth not live by bread alone' will devote a large part of their
energies to worship, prayer, and numerous spiritual exercises. A
materialist civilisation will attempt to rise above 'this world' by
sending people to the moon and, generally, getting into Space. In
terms of resources and environmental impact, the former approach
is obviously much less demanding than the latter.

Present-day concern with the environment is reflecting itself in
numerous reports. Let me take as examples two highly representative semi-official documents, *Sinews for Survival* and *Pollution:
Nuisance or Nemesis?* Each of these reports opens and closes with
expressions of very deep concern. There are a number of references
to the need to 'revise our values'. The report on Pollution says that
we can—and ought to—do two things:

"First, we can strive for the widest possible understanding of our real situation (which the authors obviously feel is not being fully appreciated at present). Second, we can free our imagination from bondage to existing systems and realise that twentieth century industrial civilisation is only one, and not necessarily the best, of the many possibilities among which mankind is free to choose."

One might have wished that the authors had pursued their line of thought a bit further and explained *why* they felt that our civilisation, which is evidently in process of conquering the whole world, is 'not necessarily the best' and *what* some of the other 'many possibilities' might be. But they do not do so. They ask for 'new values' but do not tell is which of our current values to abandon, where to find new values, and how to set about getting rid of the former and establishing the latter. The recommendations put forward in both these reports are exclusively of a technical or administrative kind, with many requests for more research and more investigations. Even if all their recommendations were faithfully implemented, this could not possibly produce 'new values' or a 'system' significantly different from what the authors call 'twentieth century industrial civilisation'.

The implementation of the modern, western life-style is of course still highly imperfect and there are many technical faults which can and should be eliminated. But it is not these faults which produce the environmental problems and dangers; they may exacerbate them; they may have the effect of reducing the so-called 'quality of life' in various respects; they may lead to quite unnecessary damage and quite unpardonable waste. But all this is purely marginal. As one of the reports quite clearly recognises: 'These steps. . . buy time during which technologically developed societies have an opportunity to revise their values and to change their political objectives'. It would be of little use if we made great efforts to buy time but then found we had no idea of how to use it.

Both reports show that their authors have an implicit belief in education—education 'in craftsmanship, in the creative use of leisure, in good-neighbourliness, good husbandry and good housekeeping' (*Sinews for Survival*). 'We hope, says the report on Pollution, 'that society will be educated and informed. . . so that pollution may be brought under control and mankind's population and consumption of resources be steered towards a permanent and sustainable equilibrium'. No doubt, education, in the widest sense of the word, is the only really effective agent of change, and there is today a wide-spread tendency to treat it, as it were, as the residual legatee of all society's problems. It is necessary, however, to ask whether education is intended merely to help people to understand problems and somehow live with them, or whether it is designed to change people's fundamental outlook and aspirations so that the problems do not arise in the first place. In order to solve a problem by education, the educators must know not only the causes but also the remedies: merely to inform people that a problem exists and to habituate them to it, is of very little use.

The volume of education has increased and continues to increase, yet so do pollution, exhaustion of resources, and the dangers of ecological catastrophe. If still more education is to save us, it would have to be education of a somewhat different kind: an education that takes us into the depth of things and does not spend itself in an ever-extending battle with symptoms.

The problem posed by environmental deterioration is not primarily a technical problem; if it were, it would not have arisen in its acutest form in the technologically most advanced societies. It does not stem from scientific or technical incompetence, or from insufficient scientific education, or from a lack of information, or from any shortage of trained manpower, or lack of money for research. It stems from the life-style of the modern world, which in turn arises from its most basic beliefs—its metaphysics, if you like, or its religion.

The whole of human life, it might be said, is a dialogue between us and our environment, a sequence of questions and responses. We pose questions to the universe by what we do, and the universe, by its response, informs us of whether our actions fit into its laws or not. Small transgressions evoke limited or mild responses; large transgressions evoke general, threatening, and possibly violent responses. The very universality of the environmental crisis indicates the universality of our transgressions. It is the philosophy— or metaphysic—of materialism which is being challenged, and the challenge comes not from a few saints and sages, but from the environment. This is a new situation. At all times, in all societies, the saints and sages have warned against materialism and pleaded for a more realistic order of priorities. The languages have differed, the symbols have varied, but the essential message has always been the same—in modern terms: Get your priorities right; in Christian terms: 'Seek ye first the kingdom of God, and all these things (the material things which you also need) shall be added unto you'. They shall be *added*, we have always been told—added here on earth when we need them, not simply in an afterlife beyond our imagination.

Today, the same message reaches us from the universe itself. It speaks the language of pollution, exhaustion, breakdown, over-population, and also terrorism, genocide, drug addiction,, and so forth. It is unlikely that the destructive forces which the materialist philosophy has unleashed can be 'brought under control' simply by mobilising more resources—of wealth, education and research—to fight pollution, to preserve wildlife, to discover new sources of energy, and to arrive at more effective agreements on peaceful co-existence. Everything points to the fact that what is most needed today is a revision of the ends which all our efforts are meant to serve. And this implies that above all else we need the development of a life-style which accords to material things their proper, legiti-mate place, which is secondary and not primary. The chance of mitigating the rate of resource depletion or of bringing harmony into the relationship between people and their environment is non-existent as long as there is no idea anywhere of a *life-style which treats Enough as good and More-than-enough as being of evil*. Here lies the real challenge, and no amount of technical ingenuity can evade it. The environment, in its own language, is telling us that we are moving along the wrong path, and acceleration in the wrong direction will not put us right. When people call for 'moral choices' in accordance with 'new values', this means nothing unless it means the overcoming of the materialistic life-style of the modern world and the re-instatement of some authentic moral teaching.

It is hardly likely that we of the twentieth century—more enslaved by material preoccupations than anyone before us—should be called upon to discover *new* values that had never been discovered before. Nor is it likely that we should be unable to find the truth in the Christian tradition. In fact, there is a marvellously subtle and realistic teaching available in the doctrines of the Four Cardinal Virtues, which is completely relevant and appropriate to the modern predicament. Let us have a look at this teaching.

The Latin names of the four cardinal virtues—*prudentia, justitia, fortitudo* and *temperantia*—denote rather higher orders of human excellence than their English derivatives—prudence, justice, fortitude and temperance. We can see at once that *temperantia*, that is, the virtue of self-control, discipline, and moderation, which preserves and defends order in the individual and in the environment—we can see that this is the virtue most needed and at the same time most conspicuous by its absence in the modern world. Our obsession with so-called material progress, naively referred to as getting 'more of the good things of life', recognises no bounds and is thus the clearest possible demonstration of *intemperantia*. It has always been known—but who would admit it today?—that *intemperantia* leads directly to despair; it means loading oneself up with even greater burdens in the pursuit of pleasure and prestige, of which one can never get enough, because they do not satisfy but merely stupefy for a little while. As André Gide once said: 'The trouble is one can never get drunk enough.' Anguish, despair, brutality and ugliness, these are the infallible signs of *intemperantia*, just as health, gentleness, beauty and happiness are the fruits of *temperantia*.

Do we really want to hear about these ancient Christian teachings when we are meant to be discussing the environment? Why this old-fashioned concern about virtues, when we might spend our time productively, or at least instructively, talking about lead-free petrol, bio-degradable plastics, the safe disposal of toxic wastes, clean air and water, noise abatement, and so forth? Yet, as the real cause of our troubles is *intemperantia*, how could we hope to bring pollution or population or the consumption of resources under control, if we cannot control ourselves and are not prepared to study the question of self-control?

However, it is quite true that *temperantia*, self-control, *by itself* means nothing at all. In the old teaching it ranks fourth among the cardinal virtues, while *prudentia*—prudence—ranks first and is described as '*genitrix virtuum*', the mould and mother of all the others. Without prudence, neither temperance nor fortitude nor justice would be virtues at all. And what is prudence? It is not the

small, mean, calculating attitude of mind which has all but conquered the modern world, but a clear-eyed, magnanimous recognition of reality. And this is indeed a *moral* achievement, because it
requires that all selfish interests are silenced. Only out of the stillness of this silence can spring perception in accordance with reality. The old Christian teaching does not define the objectivity of
prudence as some kind of ethical neutrality. On the contrary, the
cardinal virtue of prudence presupposes an orientation of the whole
person towards the ultimate goal of life. As a recent author has put
it: 'The goals are present. No one is ignorant of the fact that he
must love the good and accomplish it. . . And there is no one who
needs to be told that he ought to be just and brave and temperate.'

Again, the question demands attention: What has all this to do
with the environment? The answer is that it has something to do
with the whole relationship between us and nature. If nature is currently telling us in her own language that we are threatening her
health and life-sustaining power, we have obviously been failing in
the virtue of prudence and have not been able to see things as they
really are. The old Christian teaching maintains that nothing
blinds the individual and destroys prudence so effectively as greed
and envy.

We are flogging the environment to satisfy greed and assuage
envy, partly because we are unable to face the problem of justice
and are seeking to side-step it. 'Why worry about distributive justice', we tend to say, 'when we can promote economic growth, so
that *everybody* will be better off?' But now we are beginning to
realise that there are limits to this kind of growth, and this means
that the question of justice can no longer be side-stepped. Is it a
question to he resolved by calculation, or is it a virtue to be learned
and practised by people conscious of their final goal? The old
(Christian teaching ranks justice as the second cardinal virtue
greater than fortitude and temperance, because, as Thomas
Aquinas put it, it not only orders man in himself but also the life
of men together.

It is useless and, in, fact, impossible to speak about the environment without considering the life of people together. We can
say: Every society, every social system, produces the environment it
deserves. I have already suggested that we can call the whole of
human life a dialogue between the social system and its environment,

and if the social system does not fit reality, the environment responds by turning sick. It is because our social system not merely neglects but actively discourages the cardinal virtues of prudence, justice, fortitude and *temperantia*, that we are in trouble with the environment. Not surprisingly, therefore, many people clamour for a different social system—and they are assuredly allowing more insight than those who merely clamour for more scientific and technical research to 'solve' the problems that face us. But it must be emphasised that just as the social system shapes the environment, so our basic philosophy shapes our social system. Unless this philosophy changes, the system cannot change in its essential nature—however much it may change in terms of the distribution of power and wealth, or in terms of structure or administrative method.

The evil power of greed and envy needs to be fought by endurance as well as by attack, and to do so is the function of the cardinal virtue of fortitude. Easy-going optimism that 'science will solve all problems' or that we can somehow achieve a social-political system so perfect that no one has to be good, is the most current form of cowardice.

Let us face it: it is easy indeed to ask for 'new values' without specifying what they are and how they are to be attained. The realisation of value is impossible without the practice of virtue. Today, it takes fortitude even to suggest that there cannot be any change for the better without a change in the every day doing of each one of us.

> Be ye doers of the word, and not hearers only, deceiving your own selves.
> For if any be a hearer of the word and not a doer, he is like unto a man beholding his natural face in a glass: For he beholdeth himself, and goeth his way, and straightway forgetteth what manner of man he was. (Jas. 1:22-24)

The environment crisis is the glass, the mirror, showing us *what manner of people we are*, and the great Christian teaching of the four cardinal virtues shows us what manner of people we could and should be. There is no trace, in this teaching, of sentimentality or pietism or life-denying squeamishness. The pleasure-principle is as far removed from it as the principle of mistrusting or denigrating pleasure.

It has become part of the conventional wisdom of today to suggest that there is a fundamental conflict between maintaining a healthy environment, on the one hand, and economic growth, on the other hand. As a result, people who are concerned over the deterioration of the environment are frequently denounced as 'middle class élitists', 'bourgeois exploiters', or whatever other terms of political abuse can be extracted from the dictionary of modern controversy. Representatives of the Third World, at the same time, declare that they would gladly trade in a bit of additional pollution for an increase of their desperately low standard of living. "Human economic misery," says Mrs. Gandhi, "is the greatest pollution of all."

There is a bit of truth in all these propositions. The kind of economic growth which has become established all over the world, mainly under the influence of capitalistic enterprise, has indeed proved so damaging to the environment that one can justly say: further growth along these lines is likely to be incompatible with human survival. And if the primary motive of conservationists were fear of what might to their own high standard of living if the Third World started successfully to copy us, then one could indeed dismiss them as élitists and exploiters. Poachers are never convincing as gamekeepers. It is also true that the 'pollution' of human misery is more offensive than the pollution of the physical environment. But it is not true that you cannot fight the former without increasing the latter.

The point is that the economic system of the modern world, when considered from the point of view of real human needs, is almost unbelievably wasteful. It devours the world—the very basis of its own existence—while still leaving the great majority of people in miserable conditions. It is safe to say that the human race has never known an economic system in which the relationship between the input of irreplaceable resources and output of human satisfaction was so unfavourable as it is now. It is this system itself—the life-style of the modern world—which is incompatible with the health of Spaceship Earth, and not simply the further growth and expansion of the system.

To replace the idea of rapid economic growth by the idea of zero-growth, that is to say, organised stagnation, is to replace one emptiness by another. The environment cannot be saved by clinging to a life-style which reduces everything (as much as ever possible) to pure quantity, systematically neglecting qualitative discrimination, and then attempting to stabilise the quantity. Such an attempt, foredoomed to failure, could merely increase the general confusion, stimulate greed and envy, and drive the victims of injustice to final desperation.

Let us hope that wiser counsel will prevail: that we find our way back to the ancient Christian virtues; that we let the teaching of them permeate the whole of our educational efforts; that we learn to subject the logic of production and of productivity to the higher logic of real human needs and aspirations; that we rediscover the proper scale of things, their proper simplicity, their proper place and function in a world which extends infinitely beyond the purely material; that we learn to apply the principles of non-violence not only to the relationships between people but also to those between people and living nature.

Vol 5 No 5, Nov-Dec 1974

Chapter 21

This I Believe

IT IS NOT AN EASY THING for me to speak about my beliefs, because I can so well remember the many years of my life when the kind of belief I hold now seemed to be a sign of intellectual underdevelopment or senility. This attitude of mine could of course be interpreted as youthful arrogance; but it did not feel arrogant. I don't suppose Newton felt arrogant when he claimed his new theories to be nearer to the truth than anything that had gone before. No, I don't think it was arrogance that made me think that at long last we had discovered the only possible method for acquiring valid knowledge—the scientific method, and that therefore people who adhered to pre-scientific faiths or beliefs were simply behind the times, to be pitied rather than despised.

I did not for a moment think that this marvellous modern discovery, the scientific method, had already delivered the goods. But I was confident it would do so in time, provided only that intelligent people will not go on wasting their time on religious mumbo-jumbo. Of course there were many gaps in our knowledge, but there was no excuse for pretending that you could fill these gaps by invoking the Almighty or consulting Revelation or engaging in any kind of metaphysical speculation. All this I firmly believed for many years.

And now? Now I believe that seeing I saw not and hearing I heard not neither did I understand. What accounts for the change? I cannot claim that there was some dramatic conversion: nor have I reason to fear or suspect that my mental faculties suddenly or gradually deserted me. No, someone suggested to me that I could greatly improve my health and happiness by devoting fifteen minutes a day to certain relaxation and concentration exercises—which were explained to me.

Fifteen minutes a day, just 1 per cent of the 24 hours! This did not seem an excessive price for what was being promised or an excessive loss if all the promises were false. Why not try it?

From then on everything began to change. Texts which for so many years had been quite meaningless began to disclose their meaning—as if someone had said "open sesame!" For instance, a text like this:

> But this shall be the covenant I shall make. . .
> I will put my law in their inward parts and write it in their hearts. . .
> And they shall teach no more every man his neighbour. . .
> For they shall all know me, from the least of them to the greatest of them. . .

How could I understand such words as long as I had no idea whatever of inward parts into which 'the law' could be put or of hearts on which it could be written? My way of living had never allowed me to discover those inward parts let alone to notice what had been put into them.

Happily, the modest practice of allowing some degree of inner stillness to establish itself—if only for fifteen minutes a day, to start with—led to these unsuspected discoveries: like a Geiger counter, the inward parts started to react and in fact *to burn* as soon as my mind found itself in contact with the real thing—what shall I call it?—with 'Truth', the Truth referred to when we are told:

> Ye shall know the truth
> and the truth shall make you free.

I had not previously known of the existence of such Truth. I had rather sympathised with Pontius Pilate when he shrugged his shoulders and asked: "What is truth?!", after Jesus had said his task was to bear witness to the Truth. Now I also remembered that Jesus had promised to 'abide' in us, in our inward parts — the existence of which, for so many years, had remained totally unknown to me.

This inner organ with its indwelling spirit of Truth is really the most wonderful thing. It tells me whether something is Truth—the truth that shall make us free—sometimes long before my reason is able to understand how it *could* be such. I then may have to work hard until I can see the rationality of such a Truth. Conversely, it often greets the most plausible and seemingly most compelling arguments which my reason produces with cold indifference, and, again, I may have to work hard until I discover the flaws in my reason's arguments.

I now also understand what was meant when Jesus talked about the Comforter that would abide with us for ever, the Spirit of Truth.

> Ye know him, he said, for he dwelleth
> with you and is in you.

The Comforter is not always very comfortable: but it is nevertheless an enormous comfort to be able to obtain some help in the awesome business of picking one's way through life, of deciding between the True and the False. Of course, I don't mean deciding between the correct and the incorrect: this we must do with our unaided reason as best we can. I mean distinguishing the True from the False with regard to the only question which we cannot side-step, about which we cannot be agnostic—the question of what to do with our lives.

What we wish to do with our lives obviously depends first of all on what we think we are. After all, 'naked apes', for instance, would naturally conduct themselves differently from the way

> a chosen generation, a royal priesthood,
> an holy nation,

would wish to conduct themselves. What are we then—naked apes or a peculiar people to whom was given

> the power to become the sons of God?

There are moments, indeed, when the idea that we are nothing but naked apes, the product of mindless evolution, appeals to me. To have no obligations, to be able just to drift along, following one's instinctive promptings, just to take things easy and make oneself comfortable—if necessary even at the expense of others: Why on earth not?—The trouble is I cannot get those 'inward parts' ever to say Yes to it. The 'Comforter', evidently, is not particularly interested in comfort.

As regards the naked ape idea, there is nothing original, difficult, or unnatural about it. All religions know about it but tell us that the human race stands infinitely high above the animals. "Human birth, hard to obtain," say the Buddhists. And Jesus tells us that we have been born, not simply from our mother's womb, but 'of the Spirit' and from above'. Our dignity derives from this high position, and *noblesse oblige*. Without accepting the obligations, one is hardly entitled to demand respect for human dignity.

Noblesse oblige. The obligations of our nobility are defined in many sacred texts; nowhere more clearly to my understanding than when, in one of the great parables, Jesus lets the King say -

> I was an hungered and ye gave me no meat.
> I was thirsty and you gave me no drink.
> I was a stranger and you took me not in.
> Naked, and ye clothed me not,
> Sick and in prison, and ye visited me not.

When the people said that they had never seen him like that, he replied—

> Verily I say unto you: inasmuch as ye did it not to one of the least of these, my brethren
> Ye did it not to me.

Nothing could be clearer—to those who can recognise this as the voice of Truth. For many years I thought it was the voice of sentimentality or poetry, or idle wishful thinking But now the Comforter inside me insists that this is indeed the truth—and thereby leaves me with a problem of truly staggering proportions. How on earth can I feed the hungry and clothe the naked? There are thousands of millions of them! Well, he also says Let not your heart be troubled, neither let it be afraid. We have also been told that we are expected to use our talents, whether they are few or many and shall be counted 'good and faithful servants' as long as we produce a surplus—so that we do not simply live and work for ourselves but also serve the rest of creation and even the least of our brethren. . . And also that my yoke is easy and my burden is light. All this I believe to be true.

Vol 7 No 1, Mar-Apr 1976

Index